୨୦The Girl on the Grill୧୨

Ron Mueller

Fiction Series
The Alex Evercrest Series
The River Front
The Girl on The Grill
Missing
Maggot
Racist
Votive Candles
Windy City
Country Road
Pool of Blood
Sins of the Daughter
Body Parts
The Skull Collector
The Vanishing
The Shadow Fighter
Moonshine
Grief's Trajectory
The Magic Touch
Northern Lights
Alex Evercrest Heroine
Alex Evercrest Collection Two
New Direction
A Family Affair
Disruption
The St. Lebuinnus Church Murder

A Brian O'Neil Novel
Hawaiian Phoenix
Moon Curser
Death Broker

The Problem Solver Series
Solutions
Drug Lords
Border Crosser
The Problem Solver Collection

The Taelo Series
Taelo: The Early Years
Taelo: The Golden Feather
Taelo: Journey of Discovery
Taelo: Dangerous Passage
Taelo: Condor Clan Slingers
Taelo: Circumvention
Taelo: The Journey of Sages
Taelo: Collection
Taelo: Future Leaders Journey

A Taelo Story:
White Swan and Quiet Pheasant
The Child's Name
Floating Cloud
Quiet Rabbit
Busy Bee
Little Otter & Talking Wren
Broken Spear
Burley Bear & Meadow Flower
Taelo Story Collection

Science Fiction

The Girl on the Grill

The Savitar Series:
    Journey's End
    Savitar
    Confluence
    Savitar Series Collection

Bram Nielson Series
    The Fold
    The Message
    Fold Wormhole
    Negative Fold
    Ripples in Time
    Bram Nielson Collection

<u>Single Science Fiction Books:</u>
    Current Past and Future
    The Event
    The Door
    Viajante 7

Ron Mueller

ঞThe Girl on the Grillଔ
By: *Ron Mueller*

Around the World Publishing LLC
Cincinnati, Ohio

Ron Mueller

This story is a work of fiction. Names, characters, places, and incidents either are products of the author's imagination or are used fictitiously. Any resemblance to actual events or locales or persons, living or dead, is entirely coincidental.

The Girl on the Grill ©

All rights reserved, including the right of reproduction, in whole or in part in any form.

ISBN 13: 978-1-68223-329-0

Distributed by Ingram
Alex Evercrest Model By: Pi03@ShutterStock
Cincinnati Scene: Nagel Photography @ShutterStock
Cover Design By: Ron Mueller

To all those striving to do their best.

Ron Mueller

The Girl on the Grill

Table of Contents

1. The End of the Day — 1
2. Samual Harrington III — 15
3. Ambition — 27
4. Witness — 39
5. Protected — 49
6. Good Wife — 65
7. Protection — 75
8. New Team Member — 85
9. Connection — 97
10. A Rebound — 109
11. Weapons — 123
12. Pursuit — 131
13. Mississippi — 149
14. Cincinnati's Annie Oakley — 169
15. The Wife and Fiancé — 199
Preview of: Missing — 173
About the Author — 201
Books by the Author — 202

Ron Mueller

1 The End of the Day

Mandy did not realize that she was about to die. She saw herself as top star potential if she could get seen. she knew she would be a top echelon actress. She had fond memories of her mother who had died when she was twelve. Her mother had always let her know how good she was in school plays and had practiced many scenes from various plays with her.

Then her mother had been diagnosed with advanced breast cancer. She died a few months later. To this day Mandy thought of her daily and almost always shed a tear.

She and her father seemed to end up in a fight every time they sat too long in the same room.

He wanted her to go to Harvard or some other Ivy league school, but she chose NYU because it was in a city where she wanted to be.

She would have preferred Berkley but got a rejection letter back when she had applied.

1 The End of the Day

She had graduated from NYU and then taken a rather low-level job out in Los Angeles so that she could audition for parts in movies. She tried to break into Hollywood, but she never landed the roles that would have given her the exposure she needed.

She decided to take a break and moved back to Cincinnati when her father offered to buy her a home in Indian Hill. She figured she could see if she could do some acting there.

She accepted an offer to be a law clerk at one of her father's old college friends. She found him pleasant, attractive, and comfortable to work around. She actually enjoyed working the cases that he secured.

Then at a party that her father gave, she was introduced to a movie director. During the party she made a point of more or less throwing herself at him. It paid off. She got a lunch date with him and things took off.

Instead of simplifying her life she also got involved with her boss. She bounced between two older men, both old enough to be her fathers.

It was not long before she realized that one affair was benign and the other was not with a movie director but with a local movie drug lord. He treated her with kid gloves but when she was around him, he treated her more like a prize catch, that he used to distract the people he was doing business with.

The day she heard him discussing a huge shipment of drugs that he was to distribute throughout the east coast was the day she decided it was time to leave.

The Girl on the Grill

She excused her, went to the restroom, and decided to use the side door and leave. She was on foot and decided to go to a friend's house that was just on the other side of the highway.

She was just closing the exit door when she heard Jerry calling her to get back in. She propped an old two by four under the door handle and began to run. She had to stop and take off her shoes so she could actually run.

She was running toward the bridge and bumped into an old bum as she headed for the bridge. She knew she was going to make it and then she heard a car squealing around the corner.

Damn, she thought and tried to speed up.

The last she remembered was getting hit by Bradley's huge fist.

The hot days of August reaching into the hundred-degree range made a roast beef and potato dinner in the air-conditioned church meeting room extra special to Johnny. His "home" in the woods next to the interstate was a piece of plastic put on the ground and folded over his sleeping bag. He was not looking forward to the hot night.

He was planning to stay and listen to the discussion on "How to improve your life" that was to be led by a church member who was a local case worker at juvenile hall. He would enjoy the coffee and cookies that he knew would be provided.

This was also a special evening because he had been able to score two new long sleeve shirts. One was plaid and the other was black. He found a black pair of jeans that fit him and a black leather fedora hat. He would have a black outfit.

1 The End of the Day

He though it appropriate; "a black outfit for a black man." He knew the hat alone was worth at least fifty bucks. When he found a black pair of dress shoes, he knew that this was his night.

He made a point of visiting several local churches that had outreach programs intended to help the homeless like him. There were only twelve homeless people in attendance. He recognized most of them but as was always the case there were a few new faces.

He could tell the new ones by the deer in the headlight kind of looks on their faces. They had hit the bottom of the social ladder, and they were scared. Johnnie thought that being scared was a good thing for them. He hoped it would get them to lean on friends and family for help and to change their situation.

He thought about his own journey to the bottom. He was an aging, black, Vietnam Veteran. His many dreams had each been summarily executed by what he knew was his own shell-shocked state that had hit him after returning from Vietnam. It had been more recently been given the name PTSD. Additionally, the inherent social bias against Black people had contributed to the slide to the bottom.

He remembered the elation of graduating high school and joining the Marine Corps to escape both his poverty and the harsh discrimination by the local white folks. He had distinguished himself in Vietnam where he earned a purple heart. Then after ten years he was informed that his PTSD made him unfit.

The Girl on the Grill

He tried to get to stay in but was rejected. He was informed that the VA would give him help as needed.

He came out ill-prepared to make his way in the civilian work force. He slowly sunk into the low end of the poverty ladder. He worked at a variety of odd jobs but never had a long term one He was proud of his honesty, his braver, and his work ethic. He struggled with his inability to work back up the social ladder.

He was not lazy. He was a good person who only had one good period in his life. This period had been when he served in Vietnam and then got duty as a pay clerk in a small Army pay center. Then after his yearly examination he had been told he was get a medical discharge.

After getting out of the service , his life experiences were up and down. He never married or had children. He could not envision being unable to support a family. He could take life at the bottom, but he could not see letting anyone he truly loved share the bottom with him.

Johnnie came out of the rumination to the present time. He took advantage of the church's bathroom where he cleaned up and changed into his new black outfit.

He put his old clothes and his new black shoes into a black plastic bag that had been handed out to hold the clothes that was selected. He had only selected the black outfit and the extra shirt.

1 The End of the Day

The folks handing out the clothes wanted to give him enough to fill the bag, but he knew better. He would need to carry everything that he possessed. He did this in a green duffle bag that was currently waiting for him in the woods on the other side of the interstate. It was already full and whatever he selected would replace some item that he owned.

Too soon the presentation was over, the coffee and cookies consumed and the invitation to leave was politely extended.

Johnnie helped put the chairs and tables into a large holding closet. He picked up the three-foot dust mop and swept up the meeting area. Everything was cleaned and put away and it was time to leave. He had milked every moment in the air-conditioned meeting area that he could.

He was given a bottle of water as he got to the door and thanked for having helped clean up the meeting area.

He politely thanked the smiling motherly looking lady and put his bag of goodies over his left shoulder and walked down the daisy edged sidewalk. It was clear to him that the flowers got watered daily. He smiled as he realized they had a better life than his.

In no hurry, Johnnie stopped to open the bottle of water before walking slowly along the avenue toward the highway.

The temperature was noticeably cooler. The humidity was high, and Johnnie knew his new black shirt was going to get sweat tested. He wished he had changed back into his old shirt and kept the shirt for another occasion.

The Girl on the Grill

He was suddenly knocked to the side by a young woman who ran by him. Her outfit was not designed to be run in. Her black skirt was bunched up almost to her waist. Her nylon stockings were bunched up to her knees.

She was barefooted, carrying her black high heels and it looked like her feet were bleeding. Her black hair and the pink scarf she had around her neck was flying out behind her.

Johnnie had just gotten out a, "Hey, where are you going?" when a car came squealing around the corner and flew past him.

He started to hurry forward toward the highway overpass.

The car passed the young woman and stopped. A huge person got out and literally slammed the young woman against the bridge wall.

Johnnie had just yelled to the thug that he should leave her alone as in horror he watched the thug pick up the woman as if she were weightless and throw her over the barrier fence onto the highway below.

Johnnie could hear the squealing of tires, a huge crash and then silence.

The thug, doing the throwing, turned and pointed to Johnnie and yelled to his partner, "Get that son-of-a-bitch,"

It was too late for the young woman. He had to worry about himself

1 The End of the Day

He wasted no time in throwing his bag and his new hat over the highway barrier fence. He was up and over it as the driver of the car backed up and illuminated him. The driver jumped out and came racing over in an attempt to stop him.

Johnnie grabbed his hat and his black bag as he ran downhill onto the highway.

As he made the highway, he saw that a semi-truck had flipped and was blocking the highway. The driver had apparently tried to miss the young woman, but she was stuck to the grill of the truck just like a butterfly. Her arms were out as if she had tried to hug the radiator.

Johnnie knew she was dead, and he was now the one that the two thugs wanted to get. He looked back to see one of them clumsily climbing over the fence.

The truck had jackknifed as the driver tried to stop.

Johnnie ran across in front of the truck and took in the body stuck on the big flat radiator grill of the truck. The blood was oozing onto the hot radiator and the smell of blood mixed with urine almost stopped Johnnie.

It brought back the memory of the bodies in the rice paddies of Vietnam after a fire bombing, but he shook it off and continued running across the highway.

"Just like a butterfly. Poor kid. He wondered what she had done. For sure, he thought she had been in the wrong place at the wrong time.

The Girl on the Grill

The truck was blocking the south bound traffic. Sirens could be heard as they came slowly down on the space between the fast speed lane and the retaining wall.

Johnnie ran past the truck and jumped the wall. He was in his element. He made it across the north bound lanes by dodging and running across the lanes as the cars whizzed past. He looked back and saw that the thug following him had stopped.

Now he only had to worry about the huge thug. The huge one would have gone across the overpass and was probably waiting for Johnnie to come off the highway.

Johnnie ran north along the embankment and the retaining wall. He had one spot in mind that from the wooded side was almost impossible to walk through. That was the case unless you were Johnnie, he mused. He was like the deer or the wild dogs who shared all the woods along the highway with him. He was even friends with a couple of the hounds.

The woods were quiet. Johnnie decided he would take a break from running. He pulled out the bottle of water and took a drink.

He kept a close eye on the highway and listened for any cars stopping on his side of the highway. "Those goons ain't about to get ole Johnnie," he thought to himself

He decided that it was a good time to get some sleep. His black bag with his old clothes and his new shoes made a good pillow. He changed into his old shirt and hung the new black one on some branches so it could dry and air out. He found a comfortable slope under some bushes and closed his eyes.

1 The End of the Day

The image of the girl on the grill of the truck kept him awake for quite some time. He wondered who she was or had been and why she was murdered.

The next morning Johnnie rescued his green duffel bag and headed for the shelter. He was going there for a decent meal, a strong black cup of coffee and a change of clothes.

The early basic meal was just what he needed.

He again wondered what the young lady had done to get herself killed. He figured it had to be drugs.

He decided it was time to get to the library and find out what was being reported in the news.

Once at the library he found a monitor that was tuned to the local news. He listened intently as the newscaster made the point that the young woman was from a wealthy family and worked for Green Housing Realty.

The owner of the company was the main suspect. A lawyer named Samuel Ellington III made a public statement about the innocence of his client.

Johnnie knew he would have to go public and let the police know they had the wrong guy.

He decided that maybe the lawyer would be a better choice. He would try that first.

Johnnie figured that the accused had gotten himself a top lawyer. He knew that his PTSD history would make him a terrible witness, but he had to set the record straight.

The Girl on the Grill

"Yea, Johnnie, you mush for brains, they will all think you're touched. They'll have a good laugh and tell ole Johnnie to go back under the bridge," he continued his musing as he left the library.

He had to do something, and he figured the lawyer would be a good start.

A few days later, as Johnnie walked down the street from the library, Mary Ellen, hot wife of Henry Rambler, the accused killer was telling Samuel Ellington III that her husband was incapable of killing anyone.

He was a successful businessman who had hired the young lady as a favor to a friend. He was not a killer but a good businessman.

She thought to herself that she had picked Samuel to represent Henry for two reasons. She had seen him in the news, and he was always the winner. Second it had crossed her mind that he would be a great conquest. He was good looking, dressed very well and had a way about him that said, "let me into your bed and you will have a great time."

The murder was a major setback in the divorce proceedings she had initiated. She was planning to take Henry to the cleaners. She had the explicit, damming pictures of Henry and his now dead young secretary. Her divorce lawyer had already drawn up the divorce agreement. She would get it all.

"I am on the verge of getting his millions and now this," she thought to herself.

1 The End of the Day

She wondered if Henry was into more than a romance with a young woman younger than his daughters.

She wondered if she had missed something, but she was sure he was not a killer.

Mary Ellen had met with Samuel Ellington several times. She had worn her best and most provocative outfits each time. She knew she turned men's heads, and she figured Samuel was no different. They were all after the same thing. It was just a matter of the right timing.

"I have an appointment to get my hair done. Get Henry out of jail. He is innocent by reason of not having the capability to kill. Is there anything else I can provide to be of help," Mary Ellen said as she stood and turned to go?

She paused to look back at Samuel. She hoped her red dress with its lowcut cleavage had caught his eye.

Her smile was aimed at Samuel, but it also reflected the thought going through her mind.

"Henry is going to pay. Pay down to his last penny for being unfaithful. I am going to continue to be unfaithful until my divorce. Then I will just continue," Mary Ellen thought as she swayed her hips as she sauntered out of the office.

She was sure Samuel was watching her ass as she slowly closed the door.

Samuel watched as the blond bombshell swayed her way out of the room.

The Girl on the Grill

<u>*2 Samual Harrington III*</u>

"There goes my reward for winning this case," he thought to himself as he turned to look at himself in the mirror and take himself in.

His mirror was to the side of his desk. He was constantly checking his appearance.

"When you are the best, you have to look the best," he thought to himself as he took in his new Stefano Breyer shoes.

This was the first day he had worn them. He knew why he had hired Linda as his secretary when she complemented him on how good the shoes looked. She paid attention to details.

Samuel needed to decide to what social function to wear his new Testoni suit.

A quick motion of his hand put the imagined out of place hair where it belonged, and Samuel turned from the mirror and walked to the door.

It was time to go get Henry released. Samuel went through his list.

Henry's alibi checked out.

His wife verified he was at home at the time of the murder.

The truck driver who hit the young woman said he saw a muscular guy standing on the overpass and Henry was anything but muscular.

Samuel knew that there was no direct evidence that would allow the police to hold Henry any longer.

When he stepped out of his office, Samuel addressed his grandmotherly support, Linda. He asked her to call ahead to the police station and find out where he could get in touch with the driver of the semi that hit the girl. He wanted her to tell them that he was walking over and would like get Henry released into his custody.

Linda was old enough to be his mother or maybe even his grandmother. Early on he had learned that having a young secretary was a problem. They could be young, ugly, and still be a problem. Linda was the best and she knew how to stay on his good side.

Linda looked at Samuel as he walked out the door. He was by far the most egotistical person she knew and one of the few people who she actually disliked. But he was paying her top dollar, and he let her do her own office management.

She knew how to manipulate her boss even as he thought of himself as superior to her. Her compliments were simply to boost his ego and when he felt boosted he always wanted to do some favor

The Girl on the Grill

Samuel looked at his reflection in the elevator mirrors on the door. He thought he cut a fine figure in his Desmond Merrion Supreme suit. The suit had set him back about the same amount that Linda had paid for her new Toyota.

"But I'm worth it," he thought and smiled to himself as he got on the elevator.

Going to the station, dealing with the police, getting mixed in with the common people all bothered him.

He decided he would need to charge more and hire other people to do all the foot work.

If not murder, then what is Henry into and how in the world did he ever manage to marry that babe and to get involved with a young woman less than half his age. Samuel wondered what it was that attracted women to Henry.

Suddenly an old black man with a Vietnam Veteran's ball cap blocked his way.

Samuel rudely called him a piece of trash and told him to get out of his way. He took in the clothes and wondered who in the world wore such used and worn clothing.

Samuel was surprised when the man in front of him spouted out that he had seen a huge thug throw the woman over the overpass fence.

Samuel was, inadvertently, slowly walking backwards as he tried to maintain an arm's length distance from the person blocking his way.

It was clear to Johnnie that the lawyer had his head up his ass. He was not paying any attention to what he was saying.

He stepped aside and the lawyer shot past him like an arrow. Johnnie knew he would have to go to the police.

The police posed a problem for Johnnie. He had been picked up several times and taken in for sleeping in the park or on some warm grate. He had never been charged. He figured the police felt sorry for his condition. He had always gotten good treatment and a meal.

There was a new policewoman that he had seen early in the morning as she rode her bike past the Library. He had followed her far enough to see her park her bike in front of the police station.

Over several weeks he had watched her drive through the downtown area with a young white man that he took to be her partner.

He would see if she would listen to him.

The next day Johnnie was out in front of the Library waiting. He spotted the bike and rider when she was a block away.

He waited until she was coming through the intersection and then called out for her to stop.

Alex spotted the older black man standing at the corner in front of the Library. He was waving at her to stop.

The Girl on the Grill

She looked around to make sure he was really alone. She would whisk by if she spotted anyone. She was bit about to fall for the old trick of one person flagging someone down so the second person could rob them.

He made sweeping gesture with his arms to indicate he was alone.

She perceived that he was sharp enough to figure out her concern and decided to stop.

She took in the Vietnam Vet ball cap. When she asked when he had served and when he had been in Vietnam, she was given the year 1968 for the TET offensive.

It all sounded right to her. It was clear that the old veteran had something on his mind. She asked what he needed.

He introduced himself as Johnnie and then asked if she knew about the young woman thrown off the interstate overpass.

She replied that it was not her case but two detectives in her unit were assigned to it and had shared a lot of the details.

She listened as Johnnie described the scene from the overpass and then the scene of the young woman stuck on the semi-truck radiator like a butterfly.

Both descriptions rang true to her. The detail about being literally stuck on the radiator had not made the news. She knew she had an eyewitness to what the two detectives were calling "the butterfly murder," standing before her.

She asked Johnnie if he would walk with her to the police station.

His reply was sure, as long as she did not turn him over to any other police person. She had to be the one that asked the questions and who kept him safe.

She was not sure she could meet his request and said so.

Johnnie responded to her that he wanted to see her try and if she failed, she would owe him at least a good dinner.

Alex took a liking to Johnnie. He seemed to be a good person, and he knew that there were limits to what she could promise.

She walked her bike from the Library to the police station. After locking her bike to the rack, she led the way to her office area. Even arriving later than normal, she was still the first one in. She knew her partner would arrive before the rest of the people in the office. He had learned that it was easier to share a cup of coffee and plan the day than to come in and immediately be asked to leave to some destination that he would learn about as they drove there.

She asked Johnnie how he took his coffee and if he wanted a donut.

Johnnie responded that he took his coffee black but his donuts with as much frosting as he could get.

There were no donuts but there was a pile of small aluminum foil wrapped sandwiches label to indicate egg, cheese, and some sort of meat sandwich. She selected a sausage one for her and took a second one for Johnnie.

Johnnie thanked her for the coffee. He commented that the sandwich was better than a donut.

The Girl on the Grill

As expected, Trey McGregor, Alex's partner was the next one in. He already had his cup and a sandwich.

He sat down at his desk and looked inquisitively at Alex.

Alex introduced Johnnie.

She then asked Johnnie to share what he had witnessed. This time she asked him to tell her about what he had been doing before and then after seeing the murder.

The fact that Johnnie had come from a church function that could easily be checked out made everything he said even more plausible. When he described the scene the day before with Samuel Ellington III, she knew he was the real thing. She had seen Samuel enter and obnoxiously demand the immediate release of his innocent client.

She saw the two detectives assigned to the case and quietly asked Johnnie to stop talking and not say a word until she said so.

Trey and Johnnie both looked around and smiled. They were waiting to see what the next steps would be.

Alex saw the boss, Bruce Johnson, carry his coffee and sandwich into his office.

She walked over and knocked. She was going to start the bargaining from the top.

The shades in the office were pulled shut. Johnnie asked if the boss was always so loud and if he always used such foul language?

Trey laughed and said only when Alex was pushing him to make some change or get involved in something that he did not want her to.

Bruce opened the door and looked out into the bull pen. He signaled to Travis and Bill to come into his office.

Trey asked if Johnnie wanted another cup of coffee and a second sandwich. He was surprised when Johnnie said yes to the coffee but asked if he could put the sandwich away in his backpack for later in the day.

The loud discussion in the office went on for another twenty minutes or so. The door opened and Alex pointed out to Trey and Johnnie and crooked her finger with the come this way sign. The smile on her faced made it clear that she had won whatever position she had proposed.

Johnnie walked in around Alex and took a seat he was pointed to. Once again, he was asked to describe the events of the evening leading up to the scene of the young woman being thrown over the overpass retaining fence. Then he was asked about what he saw on the highway and where he went afterwards.

The two detectives laughed when he described the scene with Samuel Ellington III and how he thought he was a conceited asshole. They agreed whole heartedly with the description. They both had talked about their interaction with him in the same manner.

The two were not happy about sharing the case with Alex and Trey but they were elated about having an eyewitness. Their big question was whether Johnnie could identify the two thugs.

Johnnie said he thought so but that he had never seen them before.

The Girl on the Grill

After some discussion it was agreed that Travis and Bill would interview the people at the church. They would go to the closest restaurants and bars to see if they could determine where the young woman had been prior to running to the overpass.

Alex and Trey would stay with Johnnie and get him to look through the mug shots that were in the system.

The meeting in Bruce's office ended and the two pairs of detectives and Johnnie walked into a bull pen that was full and where everyone was watching what was going on. It was clear that they all knew something different was in the making.

Alex decided that they should take Johnnie into one of the huddle rooms. They could get the mug shots shown on a big screen.

Trey asked if anyone wanted a soft drink or something else to drink. Both Alex and Johnnie chose to have a cold bottle of water.

When he returned, he listened to Alex ask Johnnie a series of questions. She was setting up a search of the data base that held all the mug shots of the bag guys.

Johnnie closed his eyes and described the huge thug that had tossed the girl over the overpass barrier. He gave the size, weight, and height. Then he added that he had seen what he now thought might be a tattoo on the left bicep.

Only six mug shots came up! Johnnie immediately pointed to the third mug shot.

Alex asked about the second thug. Johnnie again closed his eyes and gave Alex the same information, but he could not come up with a specific distinguishing feature. He thought maybe a scar on the left cheek.

This time two hundred mug shots came up. By linking the search to the positive match, the number still remained at one hundred.

Alex looked to Trey and asked where he had planned to have lunch.

Trey had forgotten that it was his turn to choose the type of lunch they would experience. The two of them had tried every lunch spot in the city at least once. He looked at Johnnie and told him that lunch was on the department and asked where he wanted to go.

Johnnie beamed a smile as he automatically replied, "I've been wanting to try Scotto, but I haven't had the money to do so." "Is that place OK?"

Alex smiled and replied that it was a great place and OK. Since the lunch budget had a limit of twenty-five dollars, she knew she would have to pick up anything over that.

They walked to Scotto and were escorted to a table at the back. It was exactly what Alex wanted. She wanted her back to the wall. She felt a little like a sherif in the old west.

She accepted the menu and asked if everyone would want to have some goat cheese and hazelnut bruschetta. This was one of her favorites. Trey and Johnnie both said sure they would try it.

The Girl on the Grill

She placed the order and was pleased that all three of them had settled on water to drink. She had been afraid that Johnnie might want a cocktail or wine. She should have known better.

Johnnie was looking over the menu and commenting that Scotto's must be proud of their food because it seemed expensive to him.

Alex chuckled and added that they should be proud of their food because everything she had ever eaten at Scotto had tasted great.

She went on to point out that her dream selection came close to one hundred dollars per person. She was saving that meal for the time she could bring in that special person she was looking for.

They were enjoying the bruschetta and making small talk when Johnnie quietly said that the thug had just walked in.

Alex looked up, kicked Trey under the table, and freed her shoulder holster gun strap.

The thug looked around slowly until his eyes focused on Alex and Johnnie. Then he walked directly toward them.

Alex could see the bulge beneath his left arm and figured he was carrying a gun.

Trey was at a disadvantage since he had his back to the entrance.

Alex stood up and took one step away from the table when it was clear he was coming to their table.

She identified herself as a police officer and told him to stop.

Instead, the thug seemed to take a longer step as he reached in toward his gun.

Alex reached for her gun. It seemed to take a lifetime for her gun to leave her holster and reach its firing position between her two hands. Her finger movements were slow, smooth deliberate as she fired the first shot to the left lung area. Her breathing was slow and controlled as she pulled the trigger, and the second round fired, and the bullet hit the heart area.

The huge thug went to his knees when the first bullet hit. He was raising this gun when the second bullet hit. He was pulling the trigger when his finger lost all strength as Alex's third bullet went through his brain.

She pushed the unfired gun of the brute on the floor aside with her foot. Alex found it hard to see the hole in the forehead but the missing back on the skull and the fist sized hole made it clear there was no need to check for a pulse.

She looked around at the panicking lunch crowd.

Trey was holding up his badge and loudly shouting to the restaurant clientele that they were the police. He instructed everyone to sit down and wait for the backup to show up. The police would need statements from everyone in the room.

Alex took in the bullet spray area and was glad they had arrived early and been seated in the very back. There had been no customers directly in the path of the brain splatter.

The Girl on the Grill

She had never imagined this carnage when she went to the shooting range to practice. She was sickened by the smell of blood and other smells coming from the body.

Alex looked over to Johnnie who had quietly started to eat his Fusillialla Vodka pasta. It seemed that he was totally ignoring what had just happened. He looked at her, smiled and mouthed "good job keeping me safe," then took a big bite of his pasta.

Johnnie had watched the calm nature and steady hand that Alex had displayed. He was now sure that Alex was the right person in the police department to link up with. He knew that it was not over because the thug worked for someone that was a bigger fish. He wondered who that might be. He was going to ignore the commotion in front of him and enjoy his pasta.

He looked at Alex and gave her a thumbs up and then went back to enjoying his lunch. He was looking forward to dessert.

2 Samuel Harrington III

3 Ambition

Alex looked around at the lunch patrons. It was clear that the very large brute with three of her bullets in him was dead.

She asked everyone to sit down. She looked over to Trey. He was as stunned as the rest of the people in the restaurant.

Alex was shocked, stunned but in autopilot and doing exactly what she had been trained to do.

The shooting was going to get her suspended during the internal security follow up. She knew she would be put-on desk duty. The dead guy was going to be a catalyst that would either drive everything underground or would be the cause for retaliation.

She figured, given the bold way the thug on the floor had approached her, it would be the second. She was sure that everything was going to go into an accelerated action-reaction mode.

She felt a sense of relief when the guys in blue entered and took charge of the scene.

3 Ambition

She needed to get Johnnie back to the station and get him to ID the second guy. She would see if she could find out who the two were working for. She suspected some current drug distributor. If she was wrong then given the looks of the young dead woman, maybe it was prostitution.

She had enough foresight to ask the waiter in the restaurant to doggie bag her and Trey's lunches. She knew her day had just gotten a lot longer. She would get back to lunch sometime later in the day. Her appetite had evaporated and the knot in her stomach was a signal for her to sit down and try to relax.

This was the first time she had shot and killed someone. It was much worse than she had ever imagined, and it was nothing like the scenes shown and various police shows. Those scenes were staged, and the blood, brain splatter and the odor were not part of the viewing experience.

As she thought ahead, she made a list of everyone and everything she would have to contact, and she would have to do.

Johnnie had been the start of a very different day. Getting put on the Girl-on-the-Radiator case had been a significant second difference. She had now shot and killed someone for her first time. This was as different as it could get for her. She wondered if it could get any worse.

Then she saw Bruce, her boss walk into the lunch area and knew things would most likely get even more different.

The Girl on the Grill

She watched as her boss stopped at the entrance and slowly looked around. By this time there were at least six additional police; two were women, one white and the other black, there were two white male cops and two black male cops. It was obvious that dispatch was trying to show an integrated police to the public.

The coroner and his assistants were hovering over the dead thug and preparing to move the body. The camera flashes kept triggering a reflexive twitch in Alex's hand as if she were pulling the trigger of her gun. It occurred to her that she was having some sort of after the shooting reaction.

Alex took it all in and knew that the scene was getting top, by-the-book first responder attention. This was going to make the afternoon and evening news and would most likely have national coverage.

She hoped the Chief would leverage it to move himself and the department up a few rungs.

She put her gun into an evidence bag held out by one of the white male cops. She saw him mouth, "We've got your back." She thanked him. Then she sat down and took a sip of water.

By this time Bruce came over and asked if she was alright. He smiled and said she was looking a little white. Then he went on to ask what had happened.

Alex asked Johnnie to share what he had observed. It seemed to her that he had been the most calm observer.

3 Ambition

Johnnie put down his fork and spoon and wiped the napkin across his mouth. He took a sip of his ice water before beginning a very precise description.

He began his observation by stating that back in the station they had found the mug shot of the dead person on the floor. He was Bradley Dreadnaught or at least that was what had been on the mug shot. Johnnie went on to let Bruce know that the second guy that they were looking for was probably among the more than one hundred mug shots that Alex had organized.

Alex, Trey, and he had gone out to have lunch. He explained that he had selected the restaurant because he had always wanted to try it.

The three of them had just placed their order and had the starter put on the table, when he looked up and saw Bradley enter. He said that he had quietly warned Alex.

Johnnie made the point that Alex stood up, moved away from the table to a spot that had no customers behind Bradly. She showed Bradley her badge and let him know she was a Cincinnati police officer and told him to stop.

Johnnie looked at Alex and asked if she had positioned herself in that position on purpose.

Alex nodded and replied that the Boss had always emphasized safety of the public.

Johnnie went on to describe how Bradley ignored Alex and called her a bitch and that she should get out of his way and reached to pull out his gun.

The Girl on the Grill

Johnnie now stood up and commented that Alex dropped her badge and pulled her gun from her shoulder holster. He mimicked her movement, reached under his arm, and pulled out his imaginary gun. He did so in a smooth controlled flowing motion. Then he made the comment that he had never seen such a fast but smooth draw of a gun from a shoulder holster.

Johnnie then fired his imaginary gun and said, small hole in left chest. He then fired again and said small hole in right chest and thug went down on his knees but was raising his gun to fire. Johnnie fired the third imaginary shot and sat down.

Johnnie continued by saying the thug fell at Alex's feet as if he were prostrating before his queen.

Johnnie described Alex bending down to feel for a pulse but realizing the brain cavity was empty she stood up and looked at Trey and shook her head. She then picked up Bradley's gun with a napkin and placed it on the table.

Johnnie then told Bruce that he had a professional, by the book, dead shot jewel of a cop on his team.

Bruce had listened to Johnnie and was impressed with his description of the events. He put his hand on Alex's shoulder, gave a squeeze, and said, "Good job, by the book and very professional."

He then took in the doggie bags and told Alex that he would handle the rest of the work at the restaurant. He went on to offer that she could take the rest of the day off if she needed it.

3 Ambition

Alex was surprised at her boss's calm and quiet reaction to the shooting. It was not what she had expected.

She thanked him for the offer to take the rest of the day off but said that she wanted to identify the second thug and then see if she could link it to either a local drug dealer or maybe a prostitute ring. She said she wanted to get Johnnie back to looking at the mug shots.

She looked over to Trey and asked if he was ready to leave.

As they came up from the basement seating area and walked out into the street, Johnnie grabbed her arm and told her to look at the car parked at the corner on Walnut Street. He told her it was the car used on the night of the murder.

Alex had the keys to the chief's car in her hands, but the car was facing the wrong way. She pulled out her phone and took a quick series of photos.

The coroner and his team came out of Scotto's with the dead body on a stretcher and placed it into the waiting morgue van.

The car on the corner drove slowly away.

Alex made a call to dispatch. She asked if there was any one to apprehend a dark blue, Toyota or Honda sedan. The no response did not surprise her. She had figured that almost all the available squads were all parked around her.

She made her decision to go back to the station. She pointed to the chief's car and they all got in.

She asked Trey to keep his eyes out for the car, but she figured it was long gone from the downtown area.

The Girl on the Grill

She drove into the lot and guided the car to the spot with the Chief of Police parking sign. She noticed the looks of the team in one of the returning cars.

She knew how seldom the Chief allowed some else to get into his car. For the Chief to let someone drive it was almost unheard of.

Alex took it all in. She hoped the chief's good mood would carry over for a few more days. She knew that she was the most frequent offender of the chief's patience.

She led the way into the bull pen area, took off her empty holster and put it into the side drawer of her desk. She then pointed to the huddle room that they had left almost three hours ago. All she could think of was that it was not the lunch she had planned.

"You should have shot the car a couple of time instead of taking pictures," Johnnie commented.

Alex made her hand into the shape of a gun and pointed at Johnnie and said, bang.

He chuckled and said, "Oh yea, I forgot,"

He then turned his attention to the screen and began to rapidly flip through the mug shots.

Alex had asked Trey to write up their report about the shooting.

She was searching through the data base for Bradley Dreadnaught. It turned out that his actual family name was Dillon. She then used his real name, and it was like hitting a vein of gold. Detailed information about he and his family poured in.

3 Ambition

It turned out that Bradley had been living in the western side of the Cincinnati area. He was a bouncer at one of the Westside's more popular watering holes. Across the street from the bar was a drug distribution house that had been raided several times over the years. Each time it would close for a short period but then come back to life.

A visit to the bar was in order but it could wait until she was cleared or until she could get Travis and Bill to do the field work. She knew she would be able to pass the assignment on to them. They would be eager to get into the action.

She was heating her lunch in the microwave when the two walked in. Travis made a snide comment that he had heard that you had better be fast if you pulled a gun on her. Bill gave his partner a punch.

"Hey, it was meant as a complement," Travis responded

Alex smiled at him and told him that the compliment was understood and appreciated.

She told him that for being so nice she had a great opportunity for them. She went on and told them about the connection of her dead guy and the Evergreen Brewery and Bar out on the West Side.

She asked if they would be interested in finding out who was operating the bar and to see if the drug house across the street was back in action. She also wanted to know if the girl on the radiator had been in the bar before.

Travis looked at Bill and commented that a compliment to a good-looking lady was always appropriate.

The Girl on the Grill

Bill just shook his head and told Alex that she should not feed Travis's ego.

All of them went into the huddle room to discuss the next step each team should take.

It was clear to Johnnie that Alex was now running the investigation. He was just about to suggest that they look for the car when he stopped and instead excitedly announced that he had the guy.

On the screen was the mug shot that was almost a duplicate from the picture he had in his mind from the night he had run across the I 75 north bound traffic and saw the thug stop. He did have a faint white scar along his left cheek bone. Johnnie put his finger on the screen and said, "That's him."

It was Henry Carter Smith. Alex pulled his priors up on the screen for everyone to see. Henry had been convicted for breaking and entering and sent away for five years. He got out in three based on good behavior. He then got involved with the drug trade and was next apprehended with a car loaded with heroin. This time he got fifteen years. He had been out for three years and was working for a locally known drug dealer.

Alex was now sure the lady on the radiator had been involved in some way in the drug trade.

3 Ambition

Alex suggested that Trey join Travis and Bill and go scout out the bar. She suggested they just look around, show the picture of the dead woman, and scout out the neighborhood. If they found the car, she suggested they call in for backup before trying to catch the driver.

After the three had left, she looked at Johnnie. She had decided that he needed to be protected. She could ask the chief to assign protection, or she could see if Johnnie was willing to stay in one of the holding areas for the night.

She decided to ask Johnnie what he preferred.

Johnnie listened to his options. He asked if he could get his things and bring them in. He preferred the holding area.

Johnnie smiled and asked if a pizza could be added to the deal.

Alex said OK to the pizza, but she would check out the rest with her boss.

She told Johnnie to relax, and she would return with the verdict in a few moments.

Bruce had returned and was just picking up is car keys to put in his pocket when Alex knocked and entered.

Bruce had been in law enforcement for all of his career and on the Cincinnati Force for three years and in the last two his new black female detective had provided more action than in all the previous years. She seemed to be a magnet for getting involved in serious and deadly cases.

He waited apprehensively for her to speak.

The Girl on the Grill

Alex first thanked the chief for letting her use his car. Then she asked how long her desk assignment would be. She wanted to continue on the case and being relegated to the office would be tough.

She was happy to hear that Bruce had already checked with internal affairs and had been assured that if what he had described was the case, then it would only be a few days.

She then brought Bruce up to speed on the actions the two teams were taking.

He reassured her that he was supportive of what they were doing. He expressed concern about engaging the drug arena. He wanted to check with DEA if they had any investigation going. He did not want the department crossing beams with them.

Alex asked whether she was allowed to contact DEA and discuss the matter. Bruce said that he thought that might be appropriate, but he wanted to make the initial contact.

She realized that she had been standing almost at attention. She took a deep breath and sat down.

She next brought up holding Johnnie for protection for a short time to protect him from the drug guys. She let Bruce know that Johnnie preferred staying at the police station rather than some safe house.

Bruce had been expecting anything but such a simple request. He readily agreed.

Little did either Bruce or Alex know the chaos, madness and havoc that was about to overcome the department and the city.

3 Ambition

4 Witness

Alex drove Johnnie to the Eden Park entrance and watched as he made his way into some dense woods and underbrush near the entrance. While waiting for his return, she called Trey to see what he and the other two were up to. She learned that they had linked the pub to the girl and to her boyfriend who was a regular customer. They were in the process of digging deeper when the chief had called and told them to stop. He went on to tell them to have a good evening and he would brief all of them in the morning.

Johnnie returned carrying an old fading green duffle bag with grey almost invisible lettering of US Army on its side. To Alex, Johnnie seemed happy enough and in good health. He seemed to have figured out a way to survive without having a physical home in which to live.

She thought it rather sad that a person, who had been willing to serve and die for the country, had lived such a precarious life on its edge, for most of his time. She popped the trunk to the car and watched as Johnnie threw the duffle bag in.

She drove back to the station and got him settled in. The pizza delivery came just as she was getting ready to leave. She thanked Johnnie for his offer to share but said she was ready to get back to her apartment.

It had been a long day. She was a nervous wreck. She almost decided to drive but figured that her bike ride back to her apartment and a long walk and some jogging on the tread mill would help relieve the tension that had reached a peak.

She kept her eyes out for any suspicious cars, pedestrians, or other cyclists. She felt as if she was being watched. When she got to her apartment building, she dismounted and pretended to make some adjustments to her bike. She watched as several cars went by. She wondered if she was just reacting to the day's events.

She pushed her bicycle in and got onto the elevator. On the fourth floor she pushed the bike to the far end of the hall to the corner apartment. The apartment had a great view from the small wooden porch where she parked her bike. She had rented it because of all the windows and the porch.

From the porch, she took a look down along the street. There didn't seem to be anything unusual going on. A few cars drove by on their way out toward I 71 north.

A glimmer from the parking garage across the street made her step back into the apartment. She could not see anything to indicate any unusual activity in the garage. She decided to go down to the apartment gym and do her workout.

The Girl on the Grill

She changed into some shorts and t-shirt with the word Hawaii across her chest. She laughed to herself as she looked in the mirror and the word's, "flat as a board," flashed through her mind. She turned on the TV and left the lights on. She did not like to return to a darkened apartment, and she figured the TV would make it seem that someone was in the apartment. She closed and locked the door and walked briskly to the elevator and went to the gym located on the first floor.

She got on the treadmill and began her jogging. She could feel the sweat run down the middle of her back. She had warmed up with a brisk half mile walk on an incline of twenty degrees. Then she had run for two miles and was just cooling down when the whole building shook.

She pressed the red stop button and wiped the sweat off her neck with a towel. The other three people in the gym where looking at each other wondering if there had been an earthquake.

Alex was spooked. She did not think it was an earthquake. She wondered about a ruptured gas line. If that was the case, there could also be a fire. Just as she thought of that scenario, she heard the fire trucks.

She was about to get on the elevator when two firemen rushed in and told her not to use the elevator and to get out of the building. A third fireman came in and told them they were to get out of the building. He told them that there was a fire on the fourth-floor corner apartment.

4 Witness

Alex instinctively replied that she had a fourth-floor corner apartment.

The fireman said she looked familiar and asked her name.

She replied that she as a Cincinnati Police detective and gave her name.

He said, "Oh, yea, I saw you working the crime scene of the second pencil dick murder. I recall learning that you apprehended the murder suspect and single handedly got her put in prison.

Alex followed the fireman out the door. She looked up and followed the stream of water from one of the elevated fire hoses into the hole that had once been her apartment.

She shook her head when her first reaction was to wonder what had happened to her bike. Then she thought about the glimmer that she had seen earlier from the parking garage.

She approached one of the police officers and identified herself. She explained that it was her apartment that was on fire and that she believed it had been an attempt to kill her. She asked him to call in the incident and to let her boss know what had happened.

Then she asked if a couple of the officers would accompany her to the parking garage across the street. She let them know about the flicker that she had seen earlier. She accompanied by two police officers took the elevator to the fourth level of the parking garage. It was a front row seat to the fire-fighting action taking place across the street.

The Girl on the Grill

Alex realized that her apartment no longer existed. It was a black smoldering hole. She wondered about her bike. Damn, she had loved that bike and it had cost her a small fortune. She had insurance but she was not sure it covered a bomb or rocket attack.

She and the two officers checked out the fourth and fifth level of the parking garage but found nothing.

Alex had not expected to find anything, but she was convinced that some sort of explosive had been launched from the parking garage. It was a perfect location for such an action.

She asked that the parking garage security camera footage be recovered and sent to her office.

The same two officers drove her back to the police station. They escorted her in and helped her get access to her locker. She had no identification, no badge but she did have a combination lock. When she opened it, the female cop escort that had accompanied her openly relaxed.

Alex had two changes of clothes. A blue business dress outfit and another black pants suit. She had a picture of her mom and dad, and one taken of her when she had held a press conference. She was down to just three outfits, the two in the locker and her workout clothes she was wearing.

Seeing the picture of her parents triggered her call to them. Her mother answered and asked if everything was alright.

Alex reassured her that she was fine. Then she told her about the attack, and she wanted her mother to know if she saw it on the news that only the apartment had been destroyed.

She shared the basics but deflected her mother's questions about who was behind the attack.

The not knowing bothered her and she decided to something about that.

She had just returned to her desk when Bruce, dressed in jeans and a black t-shirt rushed in. He asked if she was alright. He wondered how she had survived the bombing or however her apartment was destroyed.

Alex replied that his insistence that his employees stay fit and healthy was what had saved her. She told him that she was four floors away in the gym working out.

Bruce smiled and replied that he was glad that he was so insistent on Alex keeping fit.

She asked if he had heard about the apartments and tenants above, below, and next to her apartment.

Bruce replied that he had asked dispatch the same question and was waiting for their report. He wondered what she was going to do for the night.

Alex replied that she planned to use one of the cots in the back room. Tomorrow would be a day for her to find another apartment and go shopping for clothes. She also had to check with her insurance agent to see if she was covered.

Bruce said he would talk to HR about the bombing and find out how the department was going to handle the situation. He said that he had never handled a situation like this.

The Girl on the Grill

He said it was a serious situation, and he was thinking about having her watched by a couple of the department folks.

Alex was going to object but then thought better of it. She was on new ground and was not sure how she should act. The feeling of uncertainty was new to her. She was a rusher in, an attack-oriented action taker. She was not used to being a target.

Bruce said goodnight, see you in the morning and left the office.

Alex looked at the clock and groaned. It was only eight thirty. She decided to see if Johnnie was awake and see what he was doing.

Johnnie had figured out how to watch the television in the holding room he had been assigned. He was watching a special report on a fourth-floor fire.

Alex nodded at him and listened as the local news special report was describing the scene of the fire and that arson was suspected.

Alex figured it was more like a rocket attack versus arson. The local news had great pictures of the scene and announced that several of the residents had been taken to the hospital and had been released. There were no major injuries. All the residents described a huge explosion that rocked the entire building.

The residents in apartments adjacent to the corner apartment all reported damage that came from the shock wave from the explosion.

Initial inspection by the fire department indicated that the building structure was sound. The poured concrete design of the building accounted for the minimal damage.

Everyone had been allowed to return to their apartment.

Johnnie made some comment about the gutted, burned out apartment and wondered what had happened to that person.

Alex answered that the person in question was going to spend the night at the police station and keep him company.

It took a minute, but then Johnnie's eyes got bigger, and he asked if it was her apartment.

She responded that indeed it was. She figured the guy that had driven away from the scene of the mornings shooting had come back for her or had sent some other person to take her out.

She knew that she had been lucky.

She asked if Johnnie knew of any weapon that could have been fired from the parking garage into the apartment.

Johnie said that he was qualified on such a weapon. It was a rocket propelled grenade. The grenades came in various sizes and designs.

Sleep did not come easy. Alex kept going over the day's events as she lay on the cot in the team room. She wondered why the revenge bombing had happened so soon.

What was she stepping into? Who had that giant thug been working for? She suspected it was not someone that was local. The local drug distributor would not want to stir up trouble with the police.

The Girl on the Grill

She did not know when she had actually fallen asleep but the last look, she took at her iPhone displayed one thirty.

Getting ready for the day was not pleasant. Alex had a change of clothes but all the things that made one comfortable in taking a shower, drying off, brushing one's hair felt awkward. The shower and sink area had no privacy. She was greeted at least three times as she got ready.

Finally, Alex made it to the office area. She realized that the bombing had also destroyed her small backpack that had contained her money, credit cards and other nick-knack. She went to her desk and retrieved the emergency cash; fifty bucks she had put in an empty cigar box the chief had thrown out.

She walked down the hall and checked in on Johnnie.

Johnnie had stayed up late. He had pulled out his long-outdated computer from his duffel and had connected to the internet. He had decided to find out more about the drug trade. He had wondered how Cincinnati fit into the picture.

He had just returned from brushing his teeth and was wondering about a cup of coffee when Alex, dressed in a black pant suit over a white blouse knocked on the door and asked if it was alright to enter.

Johnnie thought she was looking sharp and very well dressed. She looked rested and her hair was just getting dry.

Her invitation to go to breakfast in the station cafeteria, though he would have preferred elsewhere, was just the invitation he had wanted to hear. He was hungry and did not relish eating the leftover piece of pizza he had carefully put in a zip lock bag.

He was eager to share what he had learned about the drug trade and Cincinnati's pivotal position.

5 Protected

The station canteen had vending machines that offered a variety of sandwiches or packaged soups. Alex seldom frequented the cafeteria because she wanted fresh food. She took advantage of coffee being available twenty-four seven and several microwaves provided a way to heat the selected item or food that she would bring in. The bar for hot freshly cooked food was open only between six to ten in the morning and then for lunch between eleven and one. The grilled food seemed to be better than what came from the vending machines and for quick lunches Alex would buy a grilled cheese or hamburger.

It was a little after seven when Alex and Johnnie entered. They both ordered two eggs over easy. Johnnie went for two sausage patties and two slices of toast. Alex went with the bacon, an English muffin and slice of cheese.

They both grabbed a cup of coffee and took a table across from the entrance.

Alex had left a note on Trey's desk inviting him for a cup of coffee. She expected him toward the end of breakfast.

5 Protected

Just after getting and paying for their orders, Bruce entered and asked if he could join them. He looked like he had not gotten any sleep.

Alex figured that Bruce had probably spent the evening and perhaps the morning getting in contact with his friends at DEA and the FBI trying to see what might be going down in Cincinnati. She was certain that she had put herself on more than a murder case. Murder for certain but perhaps right in the middle of the drug cartel trafficking action.

She was surprised when Johnnie launched into the pivotal role that Cincinnati played in the distribution of drugs. He made the point that sixty to eighty per cent of all the drugs entering the country via the Mexican border and going to the Eastern part of the US came through Cincinnati. A small percentage was distributed locally but that was the small change. Baltimore, New York, Boston, were the big three drug markets.

He figured that the girl had been killed because she knew too much. Johnnie said that he figured she had gotten cold feet and had been clumsy at trying to get out of the position she had put herself into. He conjectured that she had for certain sentenced herself to death when she ran.

Johnnie went on to say that Alex had made someone in the drug ring very mad when she shot Bradley. That was probably why her apartment was bombed.

The Girl on the Grill

Bruce commented that he agreed with the first part of Johnnie's analysis. He stated that he disagreed with the second part involving Alex.

He had been talking to all his friends in the different government agencies. After a lot of back and forth he had concluded that the apartment bombing had nothing to with the drug cartels. He speculated that it had to do with who was most affected by Bradley's death.

It was either Bradley's partner or someone close to Bradley.

Bruce asked Alex to look more closely at Bradley's history, family, and friends. He had a premonition that the bombing had to do with Bradley's death and had nothing to do with the drug business. He wanted two investigations to take place. One into the woman on the grill and one into the bombing of her apartment.

Alex said that she needed to go out and look at what was left of her apartment. She then needed to find a place to stay and to buy some clothes.

She requested permission to be armed and was told that Bruce would recommend this to internal affairs. He told her that she would have her answer within the hour. If the answer was no, he would arrange for a female patrol officer to accompany her. He wanted Trey to work with Bill and Travis until Alex had resolved her problems.

Alex thanked the chief for his support and understanding. She waved at Trey as he walked in.

5 Protected

Trey filled a cup with coffee and walked over and asked if he could sit down.

The Chief got up and told Trey that he had warmed up a seat for him and walked out of the cafeteria.

Trey looked at Alex and complimented her on looking so professional and that the suit looked good on her. He said good morning to Johnnie and then asked what the chief had been after.

Alex shared the drug flow analysis that Johnnie had done and then the part about the apartment bombing. She told Trey that she was going to be busy most of the day trying to reconstruct her daily life. She needed to get a new place to stay and enough clothes to come to work. She wondered out loud if any of her possessions had survived.

She mentioned that the chief wanted him to work with Travis and Bill on the woman on the grill murder until she was back at work.

Trey looked at Johnnie and asked what was to be done with him.

Johnnie replied that he would be happy to just stay quietly where he was. He stated that he would be glad to continue to learn more about the drug trade or sweep the floor. It didn't matter to him what he did, but he did not want to go out. He figured he was still a target.

The Girl on the Grill

Alex agreed with Johnnie and knew how he felt. She felt somewhat the same, but she was going to take control. She would find out who had bombed her apartment, and she would bring them in.

She asked Johnnie if he could help her and watched him sit up straight and smile.

Johnnie looked at Alex and asked how he could help.

Alex asked if he was willing to research Bradley's history. This was to be a job that he would get paid for on an hourly basis and he would need to agree to and sign a confidentiality agreement.

She would teach him the basics and then he would go at it on his own. If it worked out, he might get a longer-term gig.

Johnnie said sure he would help, and he didn't need to get paid.

Alex insisted that it be a business deal, or it would be no deal.

Trey took it all in and wondered what Alex was up to. He knew that she hated the time at her desk. It appeared to him that she had figured out a way to have someone else do some of her desk work.

He looked at Johnnie and told him to watch out because Alex was a devious and very conniving woman.

Johnnie smiled and replied that he knew how to handle someone like her.

Alex led the way into the work area. She accepted all the condolences by the other occupants of the bull pen as she made her way to her corner desk.

5 Protected

She pulled out a blank sheet of paper and wrote out a simple confidentiality and non-disclosure agreement and had Johnnie sign it. She told him that if this worked out, she would have HR draw up an actual contract for his services.

Johnnie simply said Ok and signed.

Alex then had Johnnie sit down and the she opened her notebook to the page where she had written how to use the departments personal information search engine. She had another page for connecting to each of the social media web sites.

Trey sat at his desk and listened as Johnnie simple stated that he got it, followed by a wow. Johnnie said that he had never had such clear instructions provided to him on how to use the internet. He suggested Alex open a blog and have people pay to learn.

The chief opened his office door and waved Alex to come in.

Alex walked into the office and knew instantly that she would not be getting her weapon back when she saw a female police officer stand up.

The chief said that he had failed to get Internal Affairs to change their minds. He introduced Abigale Lemon who would be with her throughout the day. Abigale would be her daytime escort until she was once again armed and when Alex found an apartment there would be an all-night guard at the door for that same time.

Alex thanked the chief for his efforts. She made the point that a guard outside her door at her apartment would not have stopped the rocket grenade or whatever was used to destroy it.

The chief nodded and said he understood.

The Girl on the Grill

He told her that she should consider that when she chose her next apartment.

He told her that HR had agreed to pay for five work outfits, five casual outfits and three pairs of shoes. There was more that could be accessed but they wanted to wait to see what the insurance coverage would be.

Alex looked over to Abigale and asked if she liked to shop.

Abigale answered that she was not much of a shopper, but she was pleased to have been selected to escort Alex.

Alex liked the answer and as they walked out of the office, she asked what Abigale liked to be called.

Abigail replied that she liked and was usually called Abi.

Alex walked out passed the bike rack and felt a tinge of guilt. She figured her bike had taken the full impact of the blast and was history.

She told Abi that the first stop would be the apartment to see what of her possessions might have survived. Her next stop was to see if there was another apartment available in the same building. Then she was stopping at the Apple store to get new personal computer. Then they would make her rounds of her favorite stores to shop in to see about clothes and shoes. Her last stop would be at the bike shop to see if she how much it was going to cost to replace her bike.

5 Protected

Alex drove her car into the parking garage across the street from the apartment. She parked on the fourth level and got out and looked at her apartment. She looked down the narrow space separating the apartment building from the next building and thought she saw a bike.

She went energetically down the stairs and heard Abigale tell her to slow down. She stopped at the bottom and waited for her to catch up. Then she led the way across the street to the space between the apartment building and the one next to it where she had seen the bike.

She reached down for the handlebar and moved some bricks and lumber. It was her bike. It had a few scratches, and the front wheel was bent. It was covered by ash, but it was otherwise still functional. She was elated. Somehow it had survived.

She looked at Abi and told her that their travel plans had just changed. The bike shop in Fairfield would be her first stop after they left downtown.

Alex lifted her bike clear and put the bike out on the sidewalk. She took another look at the condition of her bike. She was amazed that it had only suffered a bent front wheel from its drop from the fourth floor. She got Abi to hold one side of the handlebar, and she held the other. Together they wheeled the bike into the apartment lobby.

The Girl on the Grill

The receptionist greeted her and asked about the bike. Then she recognized Alex, and she was sorry to tell her that her that her apartment was a total wreck. She said that there were two firemen still in the building checking every nook and cranny for damage around the apartment and the adjoining rooms. They had given most of the building a clean bill of health, but they were examining the apartments that surrounded hers.

Alex asked if there were any other two-bedroom units available.

The receptionist said that there was one on the sixth floor directly above the one that had been destroyed. Alex asked if she could look at it after she went through what was left in her current apartment.

She figured that sixth floor was above the highest level of the parking garage and safer than the one she had on the fourth floor. She liked the view from her fourth-floor apartment and did not like to be bullied. She was intent on holding her ground.

She and Abigale took the elevator to the fourth floor. As they walked down the hallway, they saw a firefighter exit from the burned-out apartment and put something behind badly bent and bulging object leaning against the wall that Alex took to be the apartment's steel entrance door.

The fire fighter looked at Alex and said that the area was off limits. Alex showed her badge and explained that it was her apartment. She asked if there was anything that she could salvage.

5 Protected

The fireman explained that the two-bedroom unit was now almost only one large room. The rocket had exploded against the steel door or very near it. It had totally destroyed the laundry room and had pushed everything on that side of the apartment into the closet and second bathroom. The second bedroom was no longer there. All the windows had been blown out. The kitchen cabinets, the stove and the refrigerator had been blown into the first bedroom and the closet and the bathroom. The water in both bathrooms had sprayed out and had helped contain the resulting fire by dowsing the walls and containing the fire. The water in the kitchen area had soaked the floor and help keep the fire from getting fuel.

Alex asked again if there was anything salvageable.

The fireman's partner had joined them and pointed behind the door. He said it was an Apple computer that seemed to be in one piece. He said he was not sure it would work but it had no outside damage.

It must have fallen to the floor because there was no table or desk in the room. He went on to say that the bed had shielded the computer from the fire and most of the water the fire department had poured in.

He went on to say that there was a full, totally soaked, dirty clothes basket in the shower stall. It was full of soggy clothes, but the basket and clothes looked undamaged.

Alex asked about any kitchen ware and pots and pans.

The Girl on the Grill

The first fireman explained that the central granite top island that housed the sink and faucet had shattered and sent shrapnel through the entire apartment. The place looked like Swiss cheese with holes everywhere.

He had not checked inside the cabinets, stove, or refrigerator. He volunteered to check the fridge and put anything that had survived into a cooler.

Alex thanked both firemen and told them she would appreciate salvaging all she could. She told them that she would return later to see what she could save. She said she needed a chance to buy some clothes more appropriate for the salvage task.

She bent down and picked up her computer. She was surprised it was dry.

She thanked the firemen and led Abi up the stairs to the sixth floor.

She unlocked the door and was greeted by a familiar sight. It looked just like her old apartment. The immediate difference was that the marble counter tops were brown and white flecked with gold colored chip where her old apartment countertop was black and white grained.

She turned to Abi and said that this would be her new digs.

Abi commented that it was gorgeous, and she walked in the rest of the way to check out the apartment.

Alex had made up her mind when she opened the door that she was staying in the building. She told Abi that she was moving up in the world. Another attack and she would be at the top.

5 Protected

On the way out, Alex told Janet, the receptionist that she would take the sixth-floor unit. She asked to have her contract re-written and approved. She would return to sign the papers and to move a few things in.

She pointed to her bicycle and Abi took hold of the left handle. Together they wheeled it across the street to the parking garage and took the elevator to the fourth floor.

The bicycle mounted onto the bike rack that had been in her car's trunk. The Apple computer went on the floor in back of the driver's seat.

Alex took the opportunity to look at the sixth-floor apartment. She wondered if she could get the parking garage owner to put up a heavy chain link fence across the area that faced the apartment building. It would not stop a would-be shooter, but it would prevent anyone from launching a rocket.

Later Abi was surprised when Alex took the Glendale Milford Rd exit and went to the Goodwill store.

She said that it surprised her that Alex shopped at such a place.

Alex laughed and told Abi the outfit she was wearing had been purchased at this store. She went on to say she doubted that she made any more income than her and was always looking for a way to stretch her dollar.

She led the way into the store ready for the first round of buying replacement clothes. On this trip she was looking for clothes she could wear for the salvage work and a couple of outfits that she would wear to work.

The Girl on the Grill

She normally did not buy used shoes but on this trip, she bought one pair of sneakers that could be washed and then after she was done with the salvage work, if they had been ruined, she would dispose of them.

She had a big smile when the bag full of clothes she had selected came to a whopping twenty-seven dollars and fifty cents.

Abi had purchased several blouses and one outfit so she could help with the salvage work. She too was all smiles as she paid twelve dollars even. She commented that this trip had already made her escort assignment well worth it.

Alex turned right out of the parking lot and headed north on Reading Road, highway twenty-two. The next stop was Mike's Bike Shop about four miles north. This is where she had purchased her bike and where she came when it needed service.

The bike shop owner knew Alex and asked what had happened to her bike. She told him that it had suffered a fall and asked how much it would cost to fix the wheel and service the bike. She liked the bike shop because it did great work at a reasonable price.

She learned the bike repair would not take long, but she needed a new front wheel. She could probably pick her bike up in three days, but Mike said he would call her when the work was done. Alex thanked him and led the way back to the car.

Her next stop was the Apple store at the Kenwood shopping center. She only went to the store when it was absolutely necessary. It was usually packed with people.

As always, the place was overflowing.

5 Protected

She explained to the store representative that the computer had been in a fire and might have water inside. She wanted it checked out and if it was in working order, she needed to buy a power adapter and a mouse.

She was asked to wait a moment. Then she was surprised by having the manager come out to personally handle the situation. The young woman that had greeted her recognized her name from the news. The manager greeted her and asked about her computer. Alex explained that it had survived a major bombing and fire. She was interested to know if it was still functional.

The manager assured her that he would personally have it checked out. He asked if she would allow the situation to be used to promote the Apple brand.

She said sure but it would have to wait until after the bomber was caught and the case resolved. The manager said that he understood and that it would be no issue.

She walked out with her work ticket and a site where she could check on her computer status and with the managers assurance that he would personally give her a call.

She then told Abi that she would treat for lunch at the food court.

Abi's attitude had warmed considerably since the morning. She had been feeling let down by being put on protective assignment but now she was totally into helping Alex. She wondered what it took to become a detective.

The Girl on the Grill

They were early for lunch and the food court was just beginning to be active.

Alex decided to have a turkey and cheese sandwich on rye. This was more than her usual lunch, but she figured she would work it off doing the salvage work.

She sat down and wondered what she would recover from her apartment. She had no idea what might have survived.

She also had no idea what Johnnie had discovered.

5 Protected

6 Good Wife

Samuel grudgingly gave his keys to the parking attendant. He stood in front of an Indian Hill home that was now an Art Gallery. The invitation card to the party showed the large empty greenhouse that was now decorated to host a party was located just to the back of the house. He could see it but the route to get to it was through the main house. He was told to first enjoy a walk through the house to view the current art being displayed and then to go to the greenhouse. Samuel noted that the art was all discreetly marked with a sales price. There was nothing that interested him, and all the art seemed priced on the high side. He enjoyed the wine as he walked through but otherwise, he felt the walk through the house was a waste of his time. It was a sales gallery intended to tap the pocket of those coming to the party.

He had been invited by Henry Rambler who he had just cleared of a murder charge. It was the easiest ten thousand dollars he had made.

6 The Good Wife

Mary Ellen Rambler was hot and had made a more or less open invitation for his advances. He planned to see if that invitation was still open. Mary Ellen was good looking, but she was at the top end of the age bracket in the field of women that Samuel normally played in.

She had mentioned divorce from Henry and that she was going to get everything. The lawyer on the divorce case was an acquaintance of Samuel and he had confided that everything was valued at almost nothing and that Henry's business might even be under water. His friend went on to say that Mary Ellen had put a hold on the divorce proceedings. Perhaps she intended to play the good wife now that she might get nothing from a divorce.

He would evaluate her behavior and decide how he would play the game. He loved a good-looking woman but like a good car, the newer ones always had more features.

There were two bars to either side of the greenhouse entrance. The bar ended and a long table with a variety of hors d'oeuvre was next. Servers were circulating with a mix of what was on the table. Others were delivering drinks.

Samuel listened to as a string quartet located in the center of the greenhouse was playing some romantic melodies. He could see a band setting up their equipment at the far end of the greenhouse. He thought their sign said Hard Candy or was it, Eye Candy as he took in Mary Ellen walking toward him.

The Girl on the Grill

His reaction to an attractive woman always surprised him. He wondered if he would ever get over it. He hoped that he would not.

He said an elongated hello and told her she looked great.

He accepted her hug and enjoyed the feel of her boobs against his chest. He took this as a good sign.

Mary Ellen took his hand and led him to a chattering group of women that were laughing, taking occasional sips of wine, and pointing to various people in the growing crowd.

Mary Ellen introduced him as Samuel Ellington the third, the stud she had been telling them about. Samuel knew then that he had just been handed off to the group and that Mary Ellen was off the list. It was clear to him that she was going to play the good wife, but she was trying to set him up as a favor. He appreciated her gesture.

Mary Ellen gave him a hug and whispered that they were all his. She gave him a pat on the butt and walked away.

Samuel stepped in toward the group and engaged in the small talk and tried to get a sense of which one was the one that would make the first move and who he would be in bed with that night.

Henry had been watching what his wife was up to. He had learned from one of his friends that she had been seen with a leading divorce lawyer. He knew that Samuel was not that lawyer, but it was clear that there was something going on. He knew the game and had seen the hand off.

6 The Good Wife

He was still reeling from the death of Mandy. His romance with her had been a surprise. She was the one who had pursued him. She was the daughter of a college buddy. He had hired Mandy as a favor. His romance with Mandy had cost him the college buddy friendship and somehow, he felt guilty about her death.

He had not known about Mandy's involvement with what seemed to be the drug trade. He knew that she was into drugs, but he thought she had that controlled to a recreation level use.

He had planned the party long before Mandy's death, to raise additional funds for his business. He felt he should have cancelled it, but he desperately needed someone to invest in his business. The invitation list was slanted toward Angel Investors or anyone known to invest in small businesses.

He was working the floor. He had asked Mary Ellen to accompany him on his rounds greeting these potential investors. He knew he had a superior business, and he was running it properly. His greatest need was enough money to advertise heavily on the major Cincinnati area channels.

Mary Ellen was the eye candy for these investors. She was in her favorite tight red, low cut dress with a slit up the side that showed off her great legs.

Henry wondered why he had lost interest in such a good-looking woman. He stood still as a moment of sadness swept over him.

The Girl on the Grill

Jerry had been sent to find out what Henry Rambler might have learned from the young woman he had helped Bradley kill.

Jerry was walking around serving snacks and drinks. He knew that he was invisible to the people he was serving. He listened to the garbage talk and realized he was not going to learn a darn thing that he was interested in. He wondered why a woman half of Henry's age would go for a loser looking guy like him.

The boss was not going to like his report, but it was clear to Jerry that a guy like Henry was clueless about the drug trade. No drugs had been arranged for this party! Jerry knew that was very unusual for parties in this part of town. It said tons about Henry.

Jerry let out a groan when he saw Bradley's mother, Denise, in a waitress outfit. He had not expected to see her here. He knew she was not at the party to seek clarifying information. Jerry had told her about Bradley going into Sotto's to get the old homeless guy they had seen entering with a black female detective and another guy he took to be her partner. He had learned and shared with Denise that the black female detective had shot and killed Bradley.

At the same time, he had boasted that he had enough weaponry to take on the entire Cincinnati police and that he and Bradley had talked about it a few times but had never acted on their verbal boasting of kicking the police ass.

6 The Good Wife

He showed Denise his armory and she had admired his grenade launcher. He found it missing the next day. He had wondered where it had gone and knew immediately when he caught the news about a huge explosion in an apartment building.

That incident had resulted in getting the Cincinnati Police department involved in his boss's drug distribution business. His boss was really angry and wanted to know if it affected him.

Jerry was also sure that Denise was now after Henry. He had learned and shared the fact that Mandy had told the boss that she was in love and that she was going to stop seeing him. Henry was the object of Mandy's affection.

The boss had been worried about what she might know about the drug distribution that he was into. When she went to the restroom and did not return to the table, the boss told Bradley to kill her. Bradley had smiled and let out a crude chuckle and replied that he would love to kill the bitch.

Jerry had seen Mandy run toward the highway and they quickly caught up with her. He had never seen anyone as powerful as Bradley. He was astonished when he saw him lift Mandy into the air and launch her over the inward curve wire fence as if he were shooting a basketball toward the hoop.

The killing would have been simple had it not been for an old black guy who witnessed the whole thing. That old guy flipped easily over the highway chain link fence and ran down past the truck that had hit Mandy.

The Girl on the Grill

Jerry ran after the old black guy and was sickened by the sight of Mandy smashed face first into the grill of a jackknifed semi. The smell made him sick. He ran past the scene and jumped the median wall trying to get close enough to shoot the old guy.

He stopped when he saw the volume of cars whizzing by. He figured Bradley would be waiting on the other side.

Bradley never saw the old guy and they left the scene as the police arrived.

They returned to the Boss and reported that Mandy was dead. They also said there had been a witness. The boss simply said for them to take care of it. Jerry and Bradley looked at each other and replied that they would.

He and Bradley had visited all the homeless shelters but failed to find the old guy. It was pure luck and bad luck for Bradley when he had spotted the old guy with the two detectives.

Bradley had told him to wait on the corner and that he would be back shortly. He told him to be ready to disappear when he came out.

Jerry never saw Bradley again. He saw the huge body bag being loaded into the coroner's van and knew that Bradley was off to see his maker.

He figured the next time he would see Bradley would be when he died and arrived in Hell.

6 The Good Wife

Seeing Bradley's mother come into the greenhouse caused Jerry slowly to move toward the food preparation area and the exit. He wanted to be able to leave the scene if Denise did anything crazy.

He was right about doing something crazy. He recognized his platinum plated fifty-seven magnum as Denise pulled it from her apron pocket and without saying a word put one bullet into Henry and another into the woman next to him. Denise calmly turned and walked toward him.

Jerry stripped off his waiter's outfit and ran as fast as he could to where he had parked his car.

He looked over his shoulder to see Denise walk into the woods and disappear.

Jerry slowly drove his car out via the entrance gate and turned to go in toward the city. He almost ran Denise over as she stepped in front of the car into the headlights.

She had a huge smile on her face as she opened the passenger door and asked where he was going and if he wanted his gun back.

No, he told her he did not want his gun back and asked if she had gone crazy.

She laughed and replied that she had probably always been a little crazy.

Jerry decided it was time to get Denise back to her home before she killed anyone else.

He responded that maybe they should go to her place in Mississippi.

The Girl on the Grill

The first shot had made Samuel duck, but he turned toward the sound. He watched as Mary Ellen was hit in the chest by the second shot.

The person doing the shooting was a rather plain looking large muscular woman. She appeared calm as she walked out of the greenhouse.

No one made a move to stop her.

He rushed forward and checked on Mary Ellen's condition. He saw what seemed to him to be a remarkably small hole between her breast but there was a huge pool of blood on the floor under her.

She was still alive and mouthed the words, is Henry OK?

He looked over at Henry and knew that he was dead, but he responded that Henry was fine. He felt the squeeze she gave his hand and watched the light go out of her eyes.

Until death do you part went through Samuels mind. In this case death more than likely had united them.

This was not what he had envisioned when he got the party invitation.

When he stood up, he realized that his Desmond Merrion Supreme suit had blood on the pants legs and there was blood on his Stefano Breyer shoes. He had blood on his hands and when he had automatically adjusted his suit when he stood up, he had blood on is shirt and jacket.

6 The Good Wife

Damn he muttered as he realized he had just destroyed the equivalent of the cost of his Tesla by kneeling down to check on Mary Ellen. "the price you pay for the attraction of a female body," went through his mind.

Samuel stood looking down at the two bodies and wondered what he had gotten himself into. He decided that he would take a trip to Hawaii and stay there for about a month or until the murders in Cincinnati were solved. He did not want to end up like Mary Ellen.

He also wondered who the shooter was and what she had to do with the entire swirling situation.

7 Protection

Johnnie quickly learned that the work of finding out about people, their action and their behavior had changed dramatically. He personally came to understand that the internet, the social media that had found a fertile home in the internet environment and the phone technology had come together to expose almost every action of most individuals. He concluded that every individual had more than fifteen minutes of fame. In fact, he felt the reverse was now true. No individual had more than fifteen minutes of undocumented time.

Johnnie prided himself as being a quick learner. He was also proud of his ability to navigate the internet. He had his own on-line internet account. He used the public library address for his home address. The Library was where he spent as much time as possible. It had comfortable places to sit and read. Tables to study on and computers for him to use. He was in the middle of studying the exploration and settling of the United States.

7 Protection

He was thrilled when Alex offered him the job to research and gather information on Bradley Dillon. The police record gave him a lot of information. He was able to access Bradley's online Google account using the police access code. Once he had that connection all of Bradley's actions and connections were open for discovery.

Johnnie got on as Bradley and began to go through the last six months of messaging. He skipped most of the back and forth messaging with individuals that were unknown. He focused on the messages between Bradley; his mother and it turned out that Bradley also had an older brother.

Bradley and his mother exchanged daily messages. There were only two messages between the brothers. Johnnie learned that Bradley's mother was in Cincinnati at the time of the young woman's killing and as far as Johnnie could tell she was still in Cincinnati when Alex shot Bradley at Scotto's.

The mother had a long rap sheet that consisted of many minor offenses of shoplifting, disorderly behavior and one of driving while intoxicated.

His brother lived in California and as far as Johnnie could tell the older brother had little to do with Bradley. The older brother's family name was Littleton. Johnnie figured that the brothers had different fathers.

Johnnie did a workup on the mother and the brother and drafted a report.

The Girl on the Grill

Johnnie watched as Trey walked in with Bill and Travis. He heard them talking about the neighborhood around the Green Leaf Tavern.

Trey came over and ask how it was going and if Johnnie was ready for lunch. Johnnie asked who was paying. He figured if the department was paying then he would get something like a soup and sandwich. He was not going to let Trey or the other two pay. When Trey said it was the department, Johnnie stood up and followed the three down to the cafeteria.

Trey answered a call, pointed to his phone, and mouthed "Alex." They talked for a while then Trey explained what Alex was up to.

Trey told the group that Alex had recovered her bike and her computer. She had called to make sure Johnnie got some lunch.

Bill and Travis laughed and asked what Johnnie had done to get Alex to pay so much attention to him. Bill went on to comment that Trey was normally ignored when it came to breakfast or lunch.

Johnnie knew how to banter and replied that he was such a fatherly figure that Alex had accepted him as one and was just showing respect.

Johnnie went on to say that he had done a workup on Bradley's immediate family. He said that Bradley and his mother were rather close. She had come to visit Bradley and was probably still in Cincinnati.

7 Protection

Johnnie enjoyed the reaction of all three detectives. He knew that they had been discounting him but now they wanted to know more. He had their full attention.

Johnnie began by sharing that Bradley had an older brother by a different father. The brother lived in Fresno, California and did not seem to be close to Bradley.

He then described the mother, Denise, as the person that must have molded Bradley and made him into what he became. She had grown up and lived all her life outside the small city of Wiggins, Mississippi. The current population of Wiggins was now around forty thousand residents. Her childhood home had been near Flint Creek Reservoir, off Oil Well road.

Johnnie had been able to get some information from social media about her. He gathered that her behavior and public life seemed to be one of getting into some legal mess about every six months. He looked her up in the police records and found that she had a long rap sheet filled with minor to major violations of the law. She seemed to have sampled a wide variety of rules to break.

He went on to describe her two marriages. Her first marriage had lasted only a little over a year. She was left with a one year old, Dennis. She remained single until Dennis was eight.

She then met, fell in love with and married Bradley's father. Denise was a strong stout, woman. She was not fat. Her second husband was large and powerful. He seemed to be all muscle. He was a heavy equipment operator.

The Girl on the Grill

Two years after they married Denise gave birth to a thirteen-pound boy. She named him after his father. Bradley was big at birth, and he grew rapidly and always exceeded the growth curve. When Bradley was two his father was killed when the front-end loader he was operating rolled over and crushed him.

Denise was devastated and she did not have the means to raise two young boys. Dennis was twelve when he went to live with his aunt on his father's side who lived in Fresno, California. This was a move that Johnnie figured saved Dennis from becoming someone like Bradley.

Bradley's actions and behaviors were clearly guided and shaped by his mother.

The e-mail exchanges between Bradley and is mother seemed to energize Bradley. These exchanges between the two occurred on a daily basis.

Johnnie commented that he figured that Bradley, a powerful hulk of a man, needed the emotional support his mother provided.

Travis asked if Johnnie knew where the mother might be staying.

Johnnie replied that he had wondered the same thing. He had made a list of hotels and motels on Cincinnati's west side that were in the area around the home Bradley rented.

Trey had been listening and now he realized that Alex had taken Johnnie seriously and had leveraged his skills. He was impressed with her insight. Johnnie had done more than any of them to keep the investigation alive.

7 Protection

He volunteered to call the hotels and motels to see if they had a Denise Dillon or any guest that was from Mississippi.

Johnnie said thanks and pushed a sheet of note pad paper to him.

Johnnie went on to say that Trey had the tone of voice and the diction that would work much better over the phone than his own high-pitched black southern twang.

Bill commented that he and Travis would begin writing up their daily report. They would stand by to see if Trey was successful in locating the mother.

He said the three could then go out to where she was staying and see if she had any information. They figured that by now she would have learned of Bradley's death.

Johnnie went back to the task he had agreed to do. This time he figured he would see who else Bradley interacted with. Perhaps he would be lucky. He was hoping to link the drug trade to Bradley's actions.

When he sat down at the computer and his fingers hit the keyboard, a new idea came to him. He decided to see what information the system had on each of the persons sitting around him and on Alex.

He decided to start with his own record.

Johnnie was pleased to find out that he was not in the police data base. He smiled about having a clean record. He had not committed any offenses that had warranted him being entered into the data base.

The Girl on the Grill

He was thorough in his search and learned that the only information on him was in the Mississippi state and county records. The last information had been his service in the Marine Corps.

He found Trey had a similar information history, but Trey was in the police data base. It turned out all police had an information sheet and personal history profile.

Johnnie learned a lot about each of the detectives. The fact that Alex was the most formally educated one of them did not surprise him. Her master's degree in law enforcement impressed him. He had been impressed with her before knowing this fact, but the information put some weight behind his feeling.

Johnnie was about to go back to researching Bradley's background and connections when he thought of the young lady that he now thought of as the butterfly on the radiator.

He decided dig into her background.

Mandy Macy Millwright was in the police data base. She had several drunk driving tickets. Each court appearance had a bigger fine than the previous one, but she had not spent any time in jail other than being held overnight in a holding cell.

She attended Cincinnati Country Day High School and had attended Notre Dame in South Bend, Indiana. She had earned a degree in Business and had been active in several clubs.

Her parents were Indian Hill residents. This indicated that the family was well to do. He wondered how Mandy had strayed so far into the drug trade.

7 *Protection*

He wondered where the family money had come from. He decided to dig a little deeper.

Deeper took Johnnie back one hundred years. His search on the family name Millwright got a hit on the history of the 1920's Prohibition period. There was a Millwright that was into smuggling rum, wine, and whiskey into the US via Mexico. At that time, the Millwrights lived in Brownsville, Texas. Across the river in Mexico was the bustling city of Matamoros.

Johnnie went to Google maps to orient himself geographically.

In Matamoros "Don Juan" Guerra established what would become the Gulf Drug cartel. He entered the booze bootlegging business in 1929 and controlled all liquor that moved across the Rio Grande into South Texas.

John William Millwright became the main distributor on the US side of the border. He and Juan became good friends as well as strong business partners. John's ability to organize the distribution of the alcohol that came across the border, freed Juan up to organize and manage the acquisition of European alcoholic beverages as well as that which was produced in various Caribbean and Latin American countries.

Johnnie learned that the majority of the distribution flow of liquor went to the US East coast.

The Girl on the Grill

John William moved the family to the Cincinnati area with the goal of better managing the distribution of the liquor. He quietly managed the business from his Indian Hill ten-acre estate. This put him outside the city into a secluded, picturesque, pleasing environment.

John paid for one of the first phone lines to be routed into the Indian Hill community. He was active in the Indian Hill politics. His immediate family never learned what he did in business, but they viewed John as a shrewd businessman.

By the time Prohibition was repealed in 1933, John had amassed a small fortune. He was not interested in participating in the next phase in the smuggling and distribution of Marijuana.

Once alcohol became legal again, it was no longer practical for criminal groups to kill or be killed over alcohol. The liquor trade went legitimate and competition between alcohol producers shifted from the bloody black market to the mainstream.

John went into the legal business of buying and distributing alcoholic beverages. His relationship with Guerra and the subsequent Gulf Cartel remained on a friendly basis until his death.

His family learned of his role in the Prohibition era only upon his death and the information John had purposely left with his lawyer.

7 Protection

Johnnie took note that like Prohibition in the 1920s, the government bans and enforcement backfired and increased the demand and increased profitability. By the 1980s, Guerra's empire had become known as the Gulf Cartel and after alcohol became legal it went into the smuggling and distribution of marijuana.

With age catching up to him by the 1970s, the drug lord named his nephew as successor. The young leadership of the cartel responded to the new trends and new drug opportunities in the underground market. This market was enriched by the War on Drugs by the Nixon administration and subsequent support and escalation by the Carter and Reagan presidencies.

Dealing in cocaine and newer drugs became more profitable as each administration escalated their effort to stop the flow of and escalated the War on Drugs.

The War on Drugs can be compared to Prohibition, in that the two episodes of history are eerily similar and quite literally related. It was Prohibition that gave rise to the Gulf Cartel it was the War on Drugs that enriched and empowered it.

A key statistic caught Johnnie's eye. The homicide rate in the US reached a peak in the final year of Prohibition but following its 1933 repeal the murder rate declined by nearly forty percent. Even if the repeal wasn't the root cause of this steep decline, Johnnie knew that this fact was too strong to be ignored.

The Girl on the Grill

He wondered if perhaps similar decriminalization and regulation of narcotics in the US would lower the crime rate around the country and bring an end to the drug war.

He doubted that he would ever see that happen.

Johnnie found it curiously remarkable that Mandy Macy Millwright had gone full circle and had reconnected with the drug business. She, however, did not have her great grandfather's business mind or a business intention.

It seemed to Johnnie that she had been attracted to the feelings that the drugs gave her.

Johnnie did one last piece of research and looked at the Indian Hill social parties that had been thrown in the previous five years. There were several reported at the Millwright home. He scoured the records for the names on the guest list.

He was surprised when he found the name Ralph Donaldson on the list. This was the person responsible for the drug distribution in the Cincinnati area.

The connection to the Millwright family and to Mandy had come full circle for Johnnie. It was probably at one of the family parties that Mandy had connected with Ralph

It had been one of Johnnie's more interesting days. He was eager to share his findings with Alex.

He looked up the format for the information reports and he asked Trey for a paper copy of an investigation report.

7 Protection

He took a break. He asked if anyone wanted any coffee. Bob and Travis both raised their hands. Trey stood up and said he would come and help carry the coffee back.

Trey asked Johnnie how he was doing.

Johnnie chuckled and made the age-old comment that he would have to shoot Trey if he told him what he had discovered.

He said he would give him a copy when he had it all written but he did not want to talk about it until Alex was in the room with them.

Johnnie knew he had discovered a totally new connection involving the lady on the grill.

8 New Team Member

The shopping center food court filled rapidly. Alex reacted every time it seemed someone was coming directly toward the table that Abi and she were sitting. She felt exposed and vulnerable. She closed the lid on her partially eaten sandwich and put the lid back on her lemonade. She apologized to Abi and asked if she minded finishing lunch at the new apartment.

Abi looked around at the growing crowd of people. She picked up immediately on Alex's discomfort. She made a comment that they should have thought of that in the first place. She put everything into a plastic bag and stood up and led the way out of the shopping center. She knew that people saw her uniform and stepped out of the way. She was not sure why people reacted that way. She hoped it was not guilt otherwise there were a lot of guilty people in the world.

It was quiet in the car as they drove south on highway 71. They took the Third street exit, and this put them one block south of the apartment.

8 New Team Member

Alex drove into the parking garage and drove up to the top level. She wanted to take a look at her new apartment. It was almost two levels above the top of the garage. This made her feel better. She hoped never to face the same situation, but she also wanted to make it harder for a shooter to shoot into the apartment. From the top of the garage if someone shot into the apartment, they would be putting holes in the ceiling.

She took the bike rack off the back of the car and put it away in the trunk. With her black bag full of clothes, she led the way to the elevator and across the street to the apartment lobby.

An enthusiastic receptionist greeted both of them. She said she was excited to tell her that the building owners had been pleased that she was staying, and they had given her a month free of rent.

She went on to say that furnishing for the apartment was being offered free of charge. The bedroom suite had already been delivered and set up. The rest of the décor needed to be selected and could be done at Alex's convenience, and the store representative was available this afternoon. If she selected items that were in the store it would be sent over in the afternoon.

Alex was surprised. She asked how much the rent would be. She asked who was providing the furnishings.

The receptionist replied that she did not know about the furnishings but that the best part was that the rent was the same as before and that the owners had said the next month was free.

Alex and Abi had the same reaction, and both said that they could not believe it.

The Girl on the Grill

The receptionist went on to say that the owners appreciated her stay on in the building. They wanted to do their part in supporting the people in the police department.

Alex asked if the building owners might own the parking garage across the street.

The receptionist said that they did not, but she knew that the parking lot owners and the building owners often had lunch together.

Alex replied that she was happy with the arrangement, but the owners would have to agree to have lunch with her at her expense. Lunch would be at Sotto's. If the garage owners attended, they could also have lunch on her.

She was planning to leverage the generosity of the apartment owners and their connection with the garage owner. She was going to go for the chain link barriers on the street side of the parking garage.

She also knew that there was an open super position for the apartment building. The super was provided a one-bedroom unit on the first floor. She was thinking this might be perfect for Johnnie.

She led the way up the stairs. Abi led out a verbal groan but followed.

Alex took the stairs with new energy. The day was turning out to be one positive event after another.

8 New Team Member

Alex opened the sixth-floor apartment and dumped her black bag on the washroom floor. She picked out her salvage outfit and shoes and threw them into the wash tub. She asked Abi if she wanted to throw her stuff in the same load.

Once the combined load was sloshing away, Alex spread her lunch out on the brown gold flecked granite. She looked into the freezer and was grateful to find a fresh bucket of ice. She refreshed her ice-tea and took a bite of her turkey sandwich.

She remembered that the bedroom was already moved in and taking another bite of her sandwich she walked around the corner into the bedroom.

The bedroom caught her breath, and she stopped in mid chew. It had a queen size bed that had a cream-colored spread on it. She lifted the spread where it went over the pillows. The sheets were alabaster colored cotton. A throw rug the same color of the spread was at the side of the bed. The cherry wood chest of drawers at the end of the bed had a deep finish that spoke of the best quality. The mirror above it reflected the face of a very surprised woman. The mirror also highlighted the ocean waves crashing into a rocky shoreline of the painting hanging on the wall behind Alex.

Abi was silent as she watched the surprised look cross Alex's face. It was clear that Alex had not expected the bedroom and furniture to be so elegant.

Alex looked at Abi and commented that she hoped that there were no strings attached.

The Girl on the Grill

Alex called the number of the decorator that was expecting to get her call.

Abi listened as Alex arranged for the decorator to come over and suggest the furnishings for the rest of the apartment. She let the decorator know that she would most likely be in the fourth-floor unit trying to salvage what she could.

Alex replied that ten minutes would be great.

She shared with Abi that she was going to see if she could find out how all this good fortune was coming about. She shared that she was having a hard time just accepting the good fortune on face value. She hoped to get more information from the sales representative.

Exactly ten minutes later the doorbell rang.

Alex opened the door to a woman that she took to be in her late forties or early fifties. She was wearing a light yellow suit with a light orange blouse. Alex wondered if she had walked over on her high heels.

The woman introduced herself as "Linda."

She invited her in and did a hand wave as she declared the apartment was all hers to decorated.

Alex waited until Linda did a walk through. Linda asked if the bedroom suited Alex.

Alex replied that it was gorgeous and done in very good taste. She asked how Linda knew that the colors and the scene in the painting were things she had always liked.

8 New Team Member

Linda replied those were the colors she had been advised to use. The painting was an original by a local painter that had been recommended on the bedroom order.

Alex asked what Linda knew about the payment for furnishing of the apartment. Linda admitted that she had wondered about that and had asked around about it. She learned that a recovery fund had been established to which people could contribute and help pay for the cost. She had found out that the main contribution had come from three sources, one in Chicago and two in Cincinnati.

Alex asked if Linda had done anything like this before. Linda said it was the first time, but she went on to clarify that she had decorated many houses and apartments.

She said she had some pictures of the furnishings, paintings, and other items that she could show Alex. If Alex agreed to the items shown in the pictures Linda would place a call, and a team would bring the items over and arrange the apartment under her direction.

Alex agreed and in less than a half hour with Linda's guidance she had selected what she knew would make her apartment a gorgeous, luxurious apartment.

As they were making the selections, Alex came across a computer desk that she preferred to have in her bedroom. The Queen-sized bed though gorgeous took up too much of the space. She asked how much trouble it would be to put in a twin sized bed.

Linda replied that it would be no problem and that she agreed that with the desk, the room would be too crowded.

The Girl on the Grill

She had engaged Abi in the selection of the furniture for the second bedroom. She was going to offer to have her sleep over for at least the next couple of weeks. She asked for the same type of desk to be put in the second bedroom.

She had learned enough that she suspected her parents of having set up the furnishing of her apartment. She placed a call to her mother.

When her mother answered her phone, Alex simply said, "Your guilty. You have the right to remain silent, but you better confess to your doings."

Her mother laughed and replied that it was the fault of a certain Northwestern Professor who insisted they pay forward the joy they had experienced in raising such an obstinate and trouble making child. He didn't see the value of waiting until he kicked the bucket to pass on some of the money Alex stood to inherit.

Alex told her mother that she loved them both and thanked them for their generosity. She thought to ask about the Cincinnati contributors. She learned that one contributor was her mother's lawyer friend from her college days. The other her mother shared was Alex's police detective partner.

Alex clarified that the apartment owners did not have anything to do with the furnishing of the apartment. She was relieved to learn that they were not.

She was surprised that Trey was involved. She asked her mother how that had happened and learned that her mother had called the department, and her boss had given her Trey's number.

8 New Team Member

He had been the source that had informed them of the total devastation of your apartment. She learned that her mother had kept him from contributing too much. She had directed him to place an order with Costco to deliver his contribution of a Lobster Tail, some scallops, and a bottle of wine when Alex called in the order.

Alex again said she loved her mother and thanked her for managing Trey and keeping him from contributing too much and that she would be able to use his contribution to host a dinner that he would be able to enjoy.

She shared what she had learned with Abi and Linda.

Abi commented that she loved her parents, but they were not in a position that they could have done what Alex's parents were doing.

Linda added that she had been asked to leave the house when she turned eighteen and that her parents would not have considered doing anything similar even if they had the money.

Alex agreed that she was very fortunate.

She decided it was time to get to the salvage work.

She and Aby changed into their salvage outfits and went down the stairs.

When they went through the hallway door and entered the fourth floor, Alex saw the yellow note on the pile outside of the apartment.

Alex picked it up and read it out loud.

"There is nothing more in the apartment. Not one dish survived. Most of the food in the refrigerator looked like machine gun victims. The stuff in the freezer survived. The clothes in the hamper look untouched.

Good luck on your recovery.

Larry and Sam

Abi looked down at her salvage outfit and said that it would make some good hiking clothes.

Alex agreed that she now had another cycling outfit. She lifted the dirty clothes hamper and the cooler. She asked Abi if she could handle the cooler. It had wheels and Abi said she would take the elevator. Alex decided on the stairs. She figured two floors was doable and no more work than carrying the hamper down the long hallway to the elevators.

Linda's crew began bringing in the furniture that had been selected.

The rich tan leather couch had reclining seats at each end. A dark mahogany end table was placed between the couch and a matching reclining chair. A glass topped oval center table sat on top of a blue and white oriental rug.

A panoramic painting of a mountainous seashore with the sun setting on the right and illuminating the mountains went across the wall opposite of the couch. Below the painting a very large, curved screen sat on a black stand. Three level high bookshelves that matched the center table were placed to each side of the screen.

8 New Team Member

The dining area behind the couch featured an oriental rug that complemented the one in the living room, but it was a light green in color. The dark glass topped high dining table was graced with four chairs to match. Linda had placed a yellow orchid at the center of the table.

Alex and Aby stood in the kitchen and sipped on ice water as they watched the transformation of the apartment take place before their eyes.

The arrival and unpacking of the dishes and pots and pans was the final surprise.

What Alex found the most satisfying was to watch each person that entered and left take out all the paper and plastic waste.

Finally, Linda announced that she was through. She asked how Alex liked her new apartment.

Alex thanked Linda and told her that she was a miracle worker. She gave her a hug and told her that she was invited to the first dinner to be held in the apartment. She asked about this coming Sunday afternoon.

Alex looked at Abi and said that the last thing they needed to do was to get their toothpaste, toothbrush, and other personal items so they could stay the night.

Alex looked over her apartment. She was exhausted from the active day and was ready for a good night's sleep.

She figured nothing was going to keep her from enjoying her new bed.

9 Connection

Alex had washed and dried all the clothes she owned. She stood in the closet and marveled that in one day she had gone from having nothing to having a fully furnished apartment, new dishes, food in the fridge, a closet with nine formal work outfits and a chest of drawer with all the basics.

She concluded that miracles did happen.

The only item left from her old apartment was the dirty clothes basket. It was a grey, fourteen by fourteen-inch hamper about three foot tall. The cooler that the firemen had left with the food that had survived was now drying out on the small porch. She planned to return it full of a variety of beer on ice. She planned to throw in a couple of extra cases of beer to make sure there would be enough for all the firefighters at the station.

As she slid into the bed, she had no doubt that she was going to have the best sleep she had ever enjoyed.

She planned to resolve the case as quickly as possible. She wanted to relax and enjoy her new place.

9 Connection

It seemed that she had just fallen asleep when she was rudely pulled up from a pleasant dream about wadding in the ocean while holding hands with the man of her dreams.

The caller apologized about the hour but there had been a double homicide with people connected with her case.

Alex was shocked by the call and more shocked by the time. She had been in bed less than two hours.

She walked out of her room and pressed the on button to the coffee pot. She was glad that she had followed her habit of having a pot ready to go at a moment's notice. She was going to need the caffeine.

She pondered waking Abi and decided that she had to because she still did not have a gun. She knocked on the second bedroom door and shared the call-in news with her.

They both dressed and carried a mug of coffee with them.

Abi followed Alex into the detective bull pen.

Trent was sitting drinking a cup of black coffee. Alex walked over and gave him a hug and thanked him for the gift.

Trent at first was going to pretend that he didn't know what she was talking about but then he decided against that. He told her that he and Lindsey had wanted to contribute more but she knew how much he got paid.

He praised the advice of Alex's mother to just give something symbolic. She was the one that had suggested the Costco food approach. Lindsey had been the one that selected the food.

The Girl on the Grill

Alex invited Trent and family to a Sunday afternoon dinner at her new apartment and said they would all share her good fortune. Then she asked about the call in.

When Alex learned who the victims were, she asked how in the world, were they connected.

She was surprised when Johnnie, who had just walked in, said he knew. He said he had heard the commotion and figured something was up.

He handed Alex his report and watched as Trey pulled a copy from his top desk drawer.

Johnnie summarized the report. The Millwright family had been connected to the drug cartel that currently controlled the Cincinnati drug scene. Mandy's great grandfather had been a distributor for the cartel during prohibition. Mandy had reestablished that connection when the local drug distributor had attended a party hosted at the Millwright estate. Johnny speculated that perhaps the presence of the drug distributor at the party indicated a reconnection of the family to the drug cartel.

Mandy's killing had been because of her falling in love with Henry Rambler.

Henry had made the news as the person Mandy had left Ralph Donaldson the drug distributor for.

Johnnie had no clue why Henry and his wife were killed or who the shooter might be. He pointed out that the woman described as the shooter sounded a lot like Bradley's mother.

9 Connection

Alex thanked Johnnie for such an in-depth research and analysis.

Alex looked at a very tired Bruce as he walked in. He asked where Bill and Travis were.

Trey responded that they were at the scene of the shooting. Trey smiled and went on to say that they had told him to stay in the office and manage the boss.

Bruce grunted and said it would take more to manage him than one white hick and sat down at an empty desk.

Alex summarized the information Johnnie had put in his research report. It seemed to connect everything in one interconnected tapestry. She handed Bruce, Johnnie's report.

A long moment of silence followed as Bruce went over the report. He looked up at Johnnie and commented that he was going to hire him to teach the rest of the department on how to write an in-depth report. He then said thanks.

He looked over at Abi and asked how she was doing.

Abi looked at him and commented that all day she had wanted to become a detective like Alex. Now she was not sure she was ready for such an assignment.

Bruce looked at Alex and asked what she thought of Abi chances. Alex looked at Abi and commented that Abi had the right attitude and she would evaluate her in the coming days.

The Girl on the Grill

She turned to Bruce and made the point that he needed to go back to internal affairs and get her reinstated for full duty. The case was about to mushroom, and she needed to be able to be fully functional.

Bruce looked around the room. He walked into his office and called them all in. He took out a new shoulder holster and pistol from the large safe in his office and formally issued it to Alex. He signed an emergency authorization and had Alex sign it as well.

He then announced to everyone in the room that he was putting Alex back on full duty and asked if there were any concerns.

He had expected none and he got no objections.

He went on to say that the paperwork and communication with internal affairs would go in at the start of the workday.

Alex thanked him for reinstating her. She figured he would face some long discussions with internal affairs.

Bruce looked at her and told her that he wanted her out at the scene of the crime and that she should "Damn well," solve the case.

Alex walked around the desk and gave him a hug. She then looked at Trey and Abi and said let's go. Johnnie asked if he could come and looked disappointed when she said he should get back to sleep or get on his computer and keep digging.

She had Trey call ahead to give Bill and Travis a heads up and that they should preserve the scene of the crime until she arrived.

She was driving but she was trying to figure out how she would unravel the case so that she could see where each thread ran.

9 Connection

She had to weave her car around several emergency vehicles before finding a place to park. The guests were still being interviewed when Alex walked into the greenhouse.

She asked Abi to find out if the number of fire trucks and other emergency vehicles could be reduced. The goal was to have one emergency vehicle and no fire trucks. She asked Trent to determine if all the police officers were needed and if the number could be reduced.

Alex walked in just as the coroner was finishing his initial assessment. He looked at Alex and commented that her cases were generating a lot of work for him.

Alex replied that in this day and age job security was a valuable commodity.

On the Pencil Dick murder case the coroner had put in a formal complaint about her compromising the crime scene evidence when she had cut the pencil in two to eliminate the tent formed at the crotch.

The Chief had taken responsibility for her action. That had been a turning point in her relationship with him.

Alex asked how the shooting had taken place.

Bill began to describe the situation, but Alex stopped him and asked if the witnesses to the scene were still available.

When they were pointed out, Alex walked over and one at a time she listened to their accounts. It always surprised her how each person saw or heard something different even though they might have been standing next to each other.

The Girl on the Grill

The shooter was consistently described as a woman in her fifties or early sixties. The gun was described as a shiny silver one and the gun shot noise had been loud enough to easily be heard over the dance music. The woman, described as the shooter, had not spoken. She had dropped the serving tray she had been carrying and pulled out the gun from her apron pocket and shot Henry and Mary Ellen at arms-length range. Everyone ended by adding, "The Ramblers were such a nice couple."

When Alex asked, she was often shown an i-phone generated picture and in one case a video shot of the crime scene. She had these sent to her email and asked the phone owner to make sure not to erase the information. She had a note entered on the list, by the names of phone owners.

The image of the shooter was caught in profile and in a full-frontal shot. Alex knew that she would have a full work up on her as soon as she got back to the office.

The coroner asked if he could take the bodies back to the Morgue.

Alex looked once again at the scene and asked about the footprint near Mary Ellen's body.

She looked over to where an emergency responder pointed.

She told the coroner he could take the bodies.

She turned to Abi and asked her to work with the police crime scene team and make sure everything at the crime scene was preserved.

9 Connection

She had been surprised to see Samuel Herrington III sitting at a table looking at his hands. He had blood on his shirt and suit sleeve and on the knees of his suit. It looked like his shoes had been cleaned off.

She walked over and introduced herself. This was the first time she had personally met Samuel.

Samuel looked at her and asked why it was taking so long to get it over with. He went on to speculate that all the incompetents must have the night shift.

Alex thought of Johnnie's description of Samuel as an asshole.

Alex smiled and agreed that all the incompetents tended to be out at night. She went on to say that it was a great night wasn't it?

She had intended to put him in the incompetents list, and she was pleased to see that Samuel seemed to get the rebuke.

Alex asked him about the blood on his clothes. She listened as he explained that he had rushed in to see if he could help Mary Ellen, but it was a futile and expensive gesture.

Alex asked him about his relationship with the Rambler's and listened as he explained that he had been hired by Mary Ellen to get Henry released from jail when he had been arrested as the murderer of the young woman killed on the interstate.

Alex knew all the details, but she wanted to hear it from Samuel. She knew that Samuel was a womanizer, that Henry had been cheating and that Mary Ellen wanted to get even. She also knew about some divorce proceedings.

The Girl on the Grill

She thanked Samuel and told him that he could leave. She asked him to stay in town until she contacted him. She had no reason to tell him that other than the fact that she wanted to cause him concern.

After talking to a few other witnesses and checking that they had all been registered, Alex released all the party goers.

Her control of the crime scene had come about in an organic fashion. It was really Bill who had the responsibility, but he had stepped back as soon as he saw how smoothly and effectively Alex went about it.

Alex was ready to return to the office. She wanted to get on her computer and find out what she could about the shooter.

Once in the office she turned on her computer and opened the messages she had sent to herself from the witness's phones.

Johnnie came in just as she put up the first picture of the shooter.

He told her that it was a picture of Bradley's mother. He filled her in on the close relationship between Bradley and his mother. When he saw the gun she was carrying, he commented that Jerry the driver of the car was a big arms collector. He speculated it was probably one of Jerry's guns.

Alex reacted to the information about Jerry being an arms collector.

Alex decided it was time to get a search warrant for Jerry's home. She wanted to see what type of weapons he might have. She asked Trey to work on the search warrant.

9 Connection

She officially entered an armed and dangerous report on both Jerry and Bradley's mother. She also had the picture of Jerry's car and the license plate number.

She asked the chief to assign Abi to also guard Johnnie. This would allow her to get him out of the station. The chief raised his eye brown, shrugged his shoulders, and muttered why not.

Alex let Abi know. She then asked Johnnie if he had a sleeping bag. When he answered that he was using it on the cot in the room he was in, she said that he was getting out of the station. Abi was assigned to guard him. She went on to say that he was probably safe, but the escort would ensure his safety.

She asked him if he would be interested in being an apartment superintendent.

Johnnie asked if it came with a place to live. When Alex confirmed that it did, he smiled and replied that he would love to have such a job.

Trey returned with a search warrant.

She asked Abi to look after Johnnie and that they were free to go wherever they wanted.

Then she and Trey left the station in her car.

The drive out I 74 took only ten minutes. They exited and drove south on Montana and then turned onto Mustang Drive to where four duel resident buildings faced each other across a large parking lot. The parking lot was empty, but each unit had a double garage facing out to the parking lot.

The Girl on the Grill

Alex turned into the parking lot and Trey read off the unit house numbers. The address they sought was for the very back unit. There was a white Subaru parked in front of the neighboring unit and a Toyota pickup parked pointed toward the street.

She parked her car so that it was in the middle of the drive with her bumper against the garage door. She wanted to keep the door from going up but if it did, her car would prevent anyone from getting a car out of the garage.

Unknown to her as she had driven west on I 74, Jerry was driving east to and then going south on I 75. He and Denise were on their way to her home in Mississippi. There was nothing for her to block in.

Alex knocked on the front door but there was no answer. Trey kicked in the door and he and Alex, with guns drawn and at the ready, rushed in.

The unit was empty. They went slowly through the entire place. The storage area to the back of the garage proved to be the highlight of their search. A long gun rack along the wall seemed to have one of each type of high-powered rifle. There were several positions on the row of rifles that were empty. The empty grenade launcher leaning in the corner brought it all into focus for Alex. The launcher she was sure was what had been used to launch a grenade or other explosive into her fourth-floor apartment.

9 Connection

She asked Trey if he wanted to bet whose fingerprints they would find on the launcher. She had little doubt that Bradley's mother's prints would be found on the rocket grenade launcher. It seemed that the mother took direct action against those she thought had wronged her.

She put in a call for backups to thoroughly go through the house.

She called the Chief and let him know what they had found. He told her that once the investigative squad got on the scene she should return to the office. He wanted to talk about what had happened over with them and let them know what he had found out.

She was now thinking about how she would pursue Jerry and Denise. She needed to determine where they might go. She and Trey had a search warrant and decided to search while they waited for the police unit that was going to process the house.

One bedroom had Denise's picture on the bedside stand. Alex figured this was Bradley's bedroom. She found a birthday card with a return address from his mother.

Home was in Wiggins, Mississippi. This is where Alex figured Denise would be going.

This helped Alex formulate her next steps and made her feel ready for whatever the Chief might throw at her and the team.

10 A Rebound

Alex walked into the office with mixed feelings. She was ninety percent certain that the attacks on her were over, at least for the near future, and she felt this applied to Johnnie as well.

She was certain her attacker had left Ohio and would be a challenge to apprehend. She understood the attack on her, but the killing of Henry and Mary Ellen Rambler seemed a senseless act of revenge.

She had resolved her feelings about her parents outfitting her apartment and accepted their generosity. She knew that she could not have handled the finances associated with being bombed out of her apartment and she had not gotten a reply from her homeowner's insurance company about coverage of her losses in her previous apartment.

She had a lunch session set up with the owners of the apartment building and the owners of the parking garage for the coming Saturday.

10 A Rebound

She wanted to thank the owners of the apartment building for their generosity, and she wanted to get the super's job for Johnnie.

She figured the heavy-duty woven wire barrier she wanted the parking garage owners to install might be harder to get agreement to, but she was going to try.

Except for Bill and Trevor, the office was empty. Bill greeted her and Trey and informed them that the Chief had everyone in the meeting hall getting briefed by the DEA on a drug investigation they were conducting in Cincinnati. He said that in light of the bombing of Alexi's apartment and the murders of the Rambler couple, they decided to raid the warehouse from where they believed the drug distribution trucking was managed. They were also going to raid the home of the person they have identified as the local drug distribution leader. The Cincinnati Police department was going to support the raids and provide scene control.

Travis went on to say that the Chief had told him and Bill that the four of them were to continue focusing on the investigation of the killing of the girl on the grill.

This seemed to Alex to be the right direction for the four of them.

She went to her computer and looked up Wiggins, Mississippi. She wondered what it would take to get local support to apprehend her attacker and killer. She hoped not to get a good old boy that would resent some northerner accusing his good folk of doing something wrong.

The Girl on the Grill

Alex wondered if she was practicing reverse discrimination or worse intellectual gratification. She asked herself, what made her assume that the local sheriff would be some uninformed country bumpkin? He would most likely be a hard-working family man. She would give whoever the person might be the benefit of her doubt and envision that person to be just like Trey.

The office began to fill. The chatter was about the upcoming drug raid that was to take place the next morning just after the first three trucks left the lot. These three trucks would be followed by the highway patrol and be allowed to go to their final destination.

Another three trucks would be in the process of being loaded when the raid took place. The Cincinnati police teams would ensure that no one left the site and then handle the detention of those that were captured.

Alex looked at the other three and commented that they were going to miss out on the fun, but they would not be playing second fiddle to the DEA or be faced with the paperwork associated with jailing all of the people that were captured.

The Chief walked in and signaled for them to follow him into his office. He made the point that the four of them were excluded from the drug raid because he wanted to see progress on what was now up to three murders and one bombing.

Alex recognized the Chief's anxiety as he ran his hand over his bald head as if it had hair. She agreed that she too wanted to see progress on the case.

10 A Rebound

She informed him about weaponry and the grenade launcher that was found in the house being rented by Jerry, the driver and Bradley, the killer. The launcher had arrived at the lab and was being examined and processed for fingerprints. She pointed out that she thought it was down to two people: the mother or Jerry. She again took the bet that it was the mother.

The Chief suggested he call the sheriff in Wiggins to ask for his help. He would make sure the sheriff knew that Denise was the primary suspect in the murder of two prominent Cincinnati citizens.

He went on to suggest that Alex and Trey plan a trip to Wiggins. If the sheriff agreed to cooperate then the two should plan to drive down in one of the units equipped to hold apprehended criminals. He pointed out that it would most likely be one of the new modified vans designed for long transport of prisoners and they would be among the first to use it.

Alex asked about the timing and the Chief told her it would depend on the sheriff, but it would probably be sometime the following week.

Alex decided that it was safe for Johnnie to leave the station. She asked him to prepare a short resume of his most significant work experiences. When he told her most of what he had done was insignificant, she told him to think about the jobs where he provided more than was expected and tell about how that was appreciated.

The Girl on the Grill

She said he should leave his duffel bag in the trunk of her car and that he should return to the station at five.

Abi asked what Alex had planned and learned that a trip to the Goodwill store was in the making. She asked about her protection duty. Alex signaled for Abi to accompany her into the Chief's office.

Alex asked about the protection and the Chief replied that once she had apprehended the killers the protection would be lifted. He went on to say that the Internal Affairs leader insisted that she get recertified to carry her gun and that she needed to attend emotional counseling.

Alex let out a little groan for theatrical effect. She actually enjoyed her chats with the department phycologist.

She returned to her desk and nursed a cup of coffee as she randomly made notes on a clean sheet of paper. She was mentally working through the puzzle about the murders and her involvement.

Johnnie came in just before the end of the workday. He said it was pouring cats and dogs as he flicked water from his hair.

The rain solidified Alex's resolve to have Johnnie stay at the apartment until she could either be successful in landing him the super's job or find some other appropriate place for him to stay.

She looked over to the spare desk that had been claimed by Abi and signaled it was time to go. Trey saw the signal and said he agreed and said he had plans to watch Planet Two with Nathan.

10 A Rebound

Alex smiled and told him he was one lucky guy to have a beautiful wife and a kid that was smarter than he was.

Trey laughed and replied that he loved her too.

As she and Abi walked out to the car, Abi commented that the two of them seemed to be really good partners.

Alex replied that yes, they were. She was especially pleased that Trey had started coming to the AA meetings with her. She had waited almost a year after her first invitation before he had decided to participate. Now she counted both of them as recovering alcoholics.

After the excitement and tensions of the last couple of days, she was ready for the AA session this coming Saturday. She laughed at herself as she thought that it was either the meeting or a drink.

The trip to the Goodwill was fruitful. Alex found an electric air pump, and a twin air mattress in almost new condition. She sent Johnnie to find a new sleeping bag and at least one work outfit that would make him look professional as an apartment superintendent. Abi volunteered to help Johnnie.

The three reconnected at the cash register. The air mattress cost twelve dollars; the sleeping bag was six dollars and the two work outfits were four dollars each. Alex was once again pleased at the low prices that she could afford.

Johnnie insisted that if he got a paying job, he wanted to pay back the purchase like it was a loan. He went on to say that if he did not get the job, "no job, no money, no repayment."

The Girl on the Grill

The next several days went by quickly. Alex followed up with the sheriff of Wiggins. She found him pleasant and very professional. She had looked him up on social media and found out the he was a veteran of Afghanistan. He had grown up in Wiggins and had been in the class two years behind Bradley. He didn't know much about Bradley because he had made it a point to stay away from the bully.

He had gone out to the Dillon house, but it looked unoccupied.

Alex thanked him and the two agreed that the sheriff whose name she had learned was James Kaizer would let her know if anyone was seen at the Dillon house.

Alex turned her attention to two personal events. She wanted to be ready to make her pitch with the apartment owners about the super's job and to the parking lot owners about the wire barriers. She had discussed this with her mother and father and had listened to their advice.

Her mother suggested introducing Johnnie to the receptionist prior to the meeting to see how the two got along and then include her in the lunch.

Her mother said that she would donate a substantial sum toward getting the chain link fence installed in the parking garage.

She made it a point to introduce Johnnie to the receptionist and she invited the receptionist to the Saturday lunch. She gave her a copy of Johnnies resume and asked her to share it with the owners.

10 A Rebound

Alex was pleased that Johnnie and Janet, the receptionist, seemed to get along. She noted that Janet commented that it would be great to get the super's job filled. She had been putting off several requests that had upset some residents.

She had also shared with her parents that she was having a Sunday house-warming dinner at the apartment. They asked if they could attend. There was no way she could refuse. They insisted that they would come in on Saturday but would stay at one of the downtown hotels.

There was no way to refuse them, and she knew that they would be more comfortable in the hotel. The weekend was getting to be a very busy one.

The manager at Scotto's was very gracious and thanked Alex for coming back and bringing a crowd. He shared that the shooting had at first caused a decline in dinner goers but had been rebounding since then. He had started to highlight the shooting event and brag about the immediate and strong police response. His approach seemed to have worked, and the business now was better than ever.

Alex greeted everyone and made introductions. She thanked the apartment owners for their great support. She thanked Janet for being so professional and efficient in managing the entire bombing event. She looked at the two parking garage owners and told them that she had a request for them, but she wanted to wait until desert to get into that discussion.

The Girl on the Grill

After drinks were served and the orders taken, Alex, once again introduced Johnnie and praised his computer skills and quick learning ability. She pointed out that Johnnie had been hired by the Police department as an information research consultant. This job, though it paid well, was unfortunately periodic in nature. He needed a solid job that would provide him a downtown residency.

She looked at the building owners and recommended Johnnie as the right person to fill the role of building superintendent that they had posted. She asked Johnnie to share the resume that he had prepared.

Alex asked Johnnie to add something of interest that was not in the resume.

He looked around at the people sitting at the table. He knew that he would be grandfather to most of them and at minimum father to the rest. He was the old guy.

He began by saying that it had been a long time since Vietnam and the journey from that time to the great lunch he was looking to enjoy today had been one of wonder and joy for him.

He said he greeted every day with a simple prayer. He prayed that he could do something good for someone that needed it, and he thanked those that had done something good for him.

He added that he was a simple hard-working person. He wanted to work and make his own way. He ended by stating they should hire him because he always delivered results.

Alex had not coached Johnnie, but she was pleased with what he shared.

10 A Rebound

She looked at the two owners and simply asked, "What do you think?"

The two owners spoke almost in unison as they said they liked the attitude of their new building superintendent.

Johnnie stood up and walked around the table to shake hands and thank them for the opportunity. Janet stood up and gave Johnnie a hug and said welcome.

Lunch arrived and conversations came to an end. A tray with wine glasses arrived with two bottles of wine. One white and one red. The wine was introduced as a gift to the table by some anonymous donors.

Alex looked at the wine and took a guess that her mother had decided to be part of the Saturday lunch. The red Sauterne and the Italian White Muscat were two of her mother's favorites, so Alex guessed that the anonymous donors were her mother and father.

She would drink her ice water, but she was pleased that her parents would be so thoughtful.

She took out her phone and sent them a thank-you text message.

The garage owners finally asked why Alex had invited them.

Alex explained that the rocket that had demolished her fourth-floor apartment had been launched from the fourth level of the parking garage. She wanted to see if she could have the garage put up some chain link fencing across the open space facing the apartment.

The Girl on the Grill

The owners agreed to having fencing put up if the city would pay the expense. They made the point that the margin on parking would not support the expense of putting up the barrier.

The apartment owners volunteered that they would contribute to the effort but wanted to see what the city response would be before committing to any specific amount.

Alex thanked them and said she would follow up with the department to get something done.

She shared that she would sleep much better if the chain link was in place and she was willing to put in her share.

The lunch had achieved the most important goal for Alex. Johnnie had been hired as the building superintended. He would have a comfortable place to live, an income and be available for her to hire as a researcher and analyst.

She walked out holding on to Johnnie's arm as he led the way back to the apartment.

She hoped that the coming week would yield as good of a result as the lunch had. She was batting .500 in the big league. She was a Johnnie Bench in the Cincinnati Police Department.

Her parents called during the early afternoon and invited her to dinner at the Montgomery Inn River Front restaurant. She walked to their hotel and together they walked down to the river front and walked along the river to the restaurant.

10 A Rebound

The fresh bread and butter and a salad was all Alex wanted. She added the onion straws on a second thought. He father went for a slab of ribs and promised her at least a taste. And her mother did the same with her order of shrimp.

Alex ordered sweet, iced tea and her parents each ordered a glass of wine.

After dinner they all walked back along the park and sat on the serpentine wall, watched the Ohio river flow by, and chatted. Both her parents were concerned about her safety. She reassured them that their daughter, though she might seem to be frail, knew how to take care of herself. She also made a point of the fact that the Cincinnati Police were among the best trained and capable police departments in the nation.

Alex walked back to the hotel with her parents and agreed to meet them for breakfast. After breakfast they would take a quick tour of Mount Adams and Eden Park. Then they would all come back to her apartment and get ready for her open house dinner.

The list had grown to include the Chief and his wife, Trey, and his family, Johnnie, Abi, Janet and her husband, and Linda the decorator and her husband and her mother's college friend. That made a baker's dozen. Alex had purchased another two lobster tails, added some shrimp and a side of salmon as the meat offering. Her mother prepared a large mixed salad, and she baked six large potatoes.

The Girl on the Grill

Her mother's friend, May, was first to arrive, and she joined in getting everything ready. Trey, Lindsey, and Nolan were the next to arrive. They were followed almost immediately by the Chief and his wife. The rest seemed to come in every fifteen minutes and Johnnie came in last.

The lunch seemed to be a resounding success; everyone commented about the delicious food and the beautiful apartment.

The desert was a pastry from Servatii Bakery and Graeters raspberry ice cream.

Alex enjoyed the gathering. Her parents and May seemed to become the center of discussion. Alex thought ahead to what the following week might hold.

10 A Rebound

11 Weapons

On Monday morning, Alex suggested they investigate the one path that they had not yet gone down. Johnnie had highlighted the Millwright family history of running booze during the prohibition era and the fact that Mandy had met Ralph Donaldson at one of her father's parties. There seemed to still be a cartel connection. She wanted to interview Mandy's father Perceval.

She asked Johnnie to do an online investigation and see what he could come up with.

Johnnie came into the station and asked if he could get on the police network. He had used the internet and the social media connections and discovered that Perceval had a financial web site, he blogged about finances, and he was fairly active on social media.

He wanted to see if there was anything on the internal police, FBI, or government websites.

By lunch time, Johnnie reported that Perceval ran a financial website designed to educate people on how to invest and a way to get their money into the funds he managed. It seemed legitimate but he had investigated a little more and found out that if people pulled their money out the buyout price was higher than the buy in price. It was legal but the price spread made it expensive to leave his fund. He made his customers money on paper, but the customer would only get half of their gains if they took money out.

This gave Perceval a solid hold on the funds he guided into his investments. It was still legal but a nasty way to do business.

On social media, Perceval displayed a negative bias to people in lower social classes. He was color blind, but he was dollar sensitive. If you had money, Perceval liked you no matter your color or origin.

Johnnie found nothing in the regular police records, but he found a DEA connection that linked the Millwright name to the Gulf Cartel. This was the same cartel that Ralph Donaldson belonged to.

It seemed that all of Perceval's work was done from his Indian Hill estate.

Alex thanked Johnnie for his thorough work. She placed a call to Perceval to arrange a meeting to discuss his daughter's death.

She and Trey drove out to Indian Hill along Given Road until they came to the address and followed a long driveway back to the Millwright home.

The Girl on the Grill

The driveway seemed to be a mile-long tree lined drive into another world. It certainly was a world that was currently beyond Alex's financial reach.

She and Trey walked up to a huge door at the front of the house and were about to ring the doorbell when it was opened by a person that spoke perfect English but with an Indian accent. They were greeted and told to come in and Mr. Millwright would be out shortly.

The home was beautifully decorated and the paintings on the wall of the waiting room were original and done by world renowned painters.

Perceval entered a short time later and introduced himself. He asked if they wanted water, coffee, or tea.

Alex and Trey both thanked him for the offer but said they were fine.

She began by expressing her condolence for the loss of his daughter.

Perceval thanked her and went on to say the news had saddened him. He went on to describe how he had purchased a home in Northern Indian Hill for Mandy to live in because she seemed to dislike staying with him. Her mother had died when Mandy entered her teen years. He and Mandy always seemed to be at odds.

11 Weapons

He was not sure how often Mandy had stayed at the house he had purchased for her but his few checks with the house maid he had hired to take care of the house seemed to indicate that of late she had spent little time at the home.

The fact that Mandy had a home of her own was new information. She and Trey would need to get a team out to the house to search it.

As Perceval shared his information, Alex was convinced he was sharing information that would lead the investigation away from him and to a focus of only Mandy.

Alex asked about his relationship with Henry Rambler.

Perceval shared that they were in the same class at Harvard. They had met each other there during the initial student orientation and had a very good relationship until just recently.

He had asked Henry to hire Mandy as a favor. He wanted to have Mandy get some work experience associated with her degree. He pointed out that even in the choice of colleges, Mandy had gone to a University other than Harvard.

He pointed out that his friendship with Henry came to an end when he found out that Henry was having an affair with Mandy. Mandy made it a point for him to know of the affair. He had wondered if she was having the affair only to spite him.

Alex had saved the question that she most wanted to ask to last. She asked how Ralph Donaldson had made it onto the guest list to a party at his house. She watched closely as Perceval stopped for a moment as if he were processing the name.

Alex took the change in the way Perceval answered as a polished lie. It was clear he was not being totally honest. He had checked with the housekeeper of Mandy's house about her use of the house and now he was acting as if he had no idea who the man was that Mandy had been seen with in his home and later for many months in bars around Cincinnati. The words liar, liar went through Alex's mind.

Alex asked directly if he knew or had done any business with Ralph Donaldson.

Percival replied that he had no idea who the man was, and he did not know of having done any business with him. but he volunteered to have his staff look into it.

Alex knew his lie was growing because Johnnie's research had discovered that Percival worked alone, and that Ralph Donaldson had been to several of Percival's parties.

Alex thanked Percival for his time, once again expressed her condolence for his loss.

Once in the car and driving back out of the lane, Alex asked Trey to get a search warrant for Mandy's home in northern Indian Hill.

Alex was not expecting much from examining Mandy's home, but she wanted to get an idea of how Mandy lived. She also wanted to talk to the housekeeper. She was just as sure that Percival would check to see if his misdirection had worked

11 Weapons

She asked Trey to call and see if they could trace the outgoing phone calls from the Millwright home from the time she had called to an hour after the time they had left.

If she could, Alex was going to unravel the lie that she had been fed.

The drive to Mandy's home took about twenty minutes.

Alex parked in the turnaround in front of the address.

She asked Trey to get a search warrant for the house and to get a team to do a thorough look through the house. She did not expect them to find out much, but she wanted to be thorough.

She placed a call to Johnnie and asked him to do some additional searches. First, she wanted to know about the house she was parked in front of. Then she wanted Johnnie to follow the Millwright money trail. She wanted to know the outgo and the income and the source of the incoming.

Johnnie said he was on it. He said he would need to get on the various systems she had access to. Alex had already given him all her access codes and said she approved of their use from her computer.

She and Trent then got out of the car and walked the lane up to the front door.

When the door opened Alex at first thought that the same housemaid had rushed up ahead of her. She showed her badge, said hello, and asked if her sister worked at Mr. Millwright's home.

The Girl on the Grill

The housemaid laughed and said yes and that they were twins. Her sister had called and said some detectives might show up. She invited them to come in.

Alex asked the housemaid to share her relationship with Mandy.

She learned that Mandy was seldom at home and was gone most of the week. She would come home sporadically but never brought anyone else home.

She asked if she could see Mandy's room.

The only picture in the room was one of her mother. It was on the bedside table.

The room seemed to be plain vanilla in its decoration. To Alex it seemed to have no character. It was a large room that made the king size bed look small. It was furnished with very good furniture, and the bed frame and canopy made the bed into a center piece. It did not have a lived-in feel. It felt like a lonely place to Alex.

Tray commented that it did not feel lived in.

Alex walked into the closet and found it held a large variety of dresses and blouses and a long three row high shoe rack with a large variety of mostly party shoes and high heels. In her view it was clearly not a working girl's closet.

She told Trey that it was time to return to the office. She thanked the housemaid and let her know that a police team with search warrant paperwork was on its way to the house to do a more thorough inspection.

11 Weapons

Once back in the office she asked Johnnie how he was doing.

He explained that the house had been built and initially owned by a hospital administrator who had retired and moved to Florida. It had stayed on the market for over a year and then had been purchased by a Perceval Millwright for one million, three hundred thousand dollars. There was nothing unusual about that transaction.

Johnnie let out small cackle and said the cash flow to and from the Millwright coffers was a spider web of cash transactions. The primary cash inflow came from two banks. One bank was in Mexico and the other bank was in Venezuela. Both were sending money to a bank account in Jamaica then it went out to a dozen directions that Johnnie had been unable to follow.

What was clear was that the cash flow streams to the blog site were all from and to US banks and they were small change compared to the cash coming out of Mexico and Venezuela. Additionally, these cash flows had periodic surges in amount but seem to happen at least once per month.

Alex decided it was time to update the Chief and see if he would link what she understood as a money laundering scheme associated with the drug cartels to the appropriate government agency.

The Chief agreed with Alex's approach and said he would get in touch with DEA to see who should follow the cash flow.

He said it was time for Alex to get on with getting the bomber of her apartment.

12 Pursuit

Alex had learned that he was a veteran of Afghanistan where he had gone for two tours of duty. He was born in Mississippi and had gone to the University of Mississippi and earned a BS in Economics. He had left the army and decided that the field of economics was no longer of interest to him. He had come home to Wiggins and on the coaching of the aging Wiggin's sheriff that at one time had coached him in soccer, he had run for sheriff and had won.

Alex found their conversation uplifting. She found it hard to keep from calling him Sheriff, even after he insisted, she call him James.

He said that he had driven by the Dillon home on Sunday evening and there were lights on in the house.

He had gone ahead and put in an arrest warrant request and a state to state transfer request. Mississippi and Ohio had a standing transfer agreement on felony level charged individuals.

12 Pursuit

Once he had these documents in hand, he would be ready to move in on the Dillon home. He said he would wait for Alex's arrival before trying to apprehend the two suspects. He wanted to apprehend Denise and Jerry early Thursday morning. He figured she would be able to make the drive back to Cincinnati on Friday.

Alex shared her conversation with the Chief and got his approval to the timing. He suggested that Abi go along and provide back up support. He pointed out that Denise had killed two people and was a dangerous character. Alex thanked the Chief and went out to bring Trey and Abi up to speed.

The three discussed the trip and agreed to leave the next day and go as far as Birmingham. Abi volunteered to find a place to spend the night. She asked if she could arrange a stay at a Bed & Breakfast instead of a conventional hotel.

Alex said she liked the idea.

Abi's selection in downtown Birmingham on Cobb lane featured a Peacock room that she assigned to Trey. The room with the Leopard pillow went to Alex and she took the pink room.

Alex arranged for the night in Wiggins. She had tried the B&B idea, but she could not find any in or near Wiggins. She chose the Hampton Inn Suites in Wiggins as the most convenient place to stay.

The three agreed on an early morning departure from Cincinnati

Abi called dibs on being the first driver. Alex smiled and agreed. She could tell that Abi was into the trip.

The Girl on the Grill

She felt somewhat the same eagerness but what waited at the other end worried her. It would be good to have some dull hours driving down to the deep south.

They had a barbecue lunch at a top Nashville restaurant and then drove on to Birmingham where they stayed at the B&B for the night. They walked to a nearby restaurant for dinner and afterwards sat out on the veranda and enjoyed an iced tea. Abi carried most of the conversation and Trey seemed to provide the leading questions that kept her talking. Alex was content to listen and sip her sweet tea.

The three of them seemed to be well matched. Trey was a good listener; Abi was into sports and related well with Alex's love for cycling. Abi made it clear that she loved to watch not to ride. They left the porch as the night closed in, and the view became that of looking at the lights of the lamp posts.

The drive the next morning from Birmingham to Wiggins seemed to take them from civilization back in time to a less populated countryside.

Alex was driving and even though she was on an interstate there were few exits and then only small towns along the way. When she drove into Wiggins and found the Hampton Inn, she felt like she had come to an oasis in the middle of nowhere.

12 Pursuit

A sheriff's patrol car was parked by the entrance, and they met James for their first time. Alex saw the reaction on his face and knew immediately that he had not known she was black. Her speech and diction were more like Midwestern white. Her mother had insisted she take speech classes and had also taken her to Toast Masters with her.

Her mother wanted Alex to learn to talk clearly, effectively and with confidence in public. Alex had excelled and won several awards for her speeches in various Toast Master competitions. She was still active in a Toast Masters club in Cincinnati. She enjoyed the meetings and giving impromptu speeches.

She stepped forward and gave James a hug. She stepped back and introduced Abi and Trey. She suggested they continue their conversation and do any required planning at dinner. She looked at James and asked where he was planning to hold their planning dinner. She made the point that he would select the food, but she would pay.

She suggested that while James figured out where to take them, they would check in and go to their rooms and then return to the lobby in fifteen minutes.

Alex took her overnight bag to her room, took a quick break and a moment to freshen up and then walked down the stairs to the lobby.

The Girl on the Grill

She was the first one back and engaged James in a conversation. She brought up his surprised look when he had first seen her and asked if that was a problem. James laughed and said no there was no issue and that his best friend since grade school was black, but he would have lost a bet if anyone had made one about Alex's heritage.

Trey and Abi came down into the lobby at the same time. James suggested the Sawmill Family Restaurant as the best place for them to discuss the upcoming raid on the Dillon home. He had called and arranged for a table that was in a back corner of the restaurant.

James asked them to follow him and walked to out his car. Alex, Trey, and Abi got into the transport van and drove south to the restaurant. The parking lot was almost empty, and the restaurant sparsely occupied. The back corner was about as isolated as it could get in an open space restaurant.

They followed James in and were escorted to a back table. It was clear that everyone knew James. He was Sheriff Kaizer to everyone that talked to him.

James waited until the drinks had been ordered and then he pulled out a house map. He said it was the building plans for the Dillon house that was on record in the county courthouse. He described each level and which bedroom Denise slept in. In preparation for the raid, he had reviewed the plans with all of his deputies. They were all ready to go.

12 Pursuit

He went on to describe how his eight deputies would be deployed. He was placing two on each side of the house. The four of them would go in rom the back through the kitchen and be backed up by the two deputies assigned to that side of the house. The rest of the deputies would stay in place on the outside of the house.

The emergency response team would be on call but would stay at the hospital.

The raid was scheduled to get underway at five in the morning.

Alex shared that she, Trey, and Abi would be in full body armor. This included a helmet and face mask. She asked if James had similar equipment.

He said that he had a helmet and face shield that he had never used and only had the standard bullet proof vest. He said he would match their precautions.

The dinner arrived and talk ended as everyone concentrated on eating. Alex would later have trouble recalling what she had ordered or eaten. Her mind was already working through the raid.

Dinner ended and once out in the parking lot he thanked Alex for the dinner and asked them to be at the station at five in the morning.

Alex drove back to the hotel and suggested they all hit the hay. Everyone would meet back in the lobby at four forty-five and go to the Sheriff's office.

The next morning, they arrived and checked in. They were offered some coffee that they all accepted.

The Girl on the Grill

James made a comment about the level of protection his Cincinnati counter parts were employing as he put on his bullet proof vest. He said they had made him decide to also use his helmet and face shield. He again admitted that he had never used it before.

Alex responded that Denise had used a rocket powered grenade launcher to totally destroy her Cincinnati apartment. This was a mad woman they were dealing with, and she was not taking any chances, and neither should he.

Alex drove the transport van. She followed James who was driving his sheriff's car. It was an eerie early morning drive out to Denise's home. Abi was riding with James and Trey was with her in the van in the passenger seat.

The depth of the darkness, the sound of the tires on the road, her dream and premonition of trouble had kept Alex up much of the night and now gave her an uneasy feeling. She made sure everyone was properly in their full body armor riot gear.

The remaining deputies, in their cars, followed in line behind the van.

James pulled his car over on the shoulder and Alex parked behind him. The rest of the deputies lined up behind the van. They had stopped roughly a quarter of a mile from the house.

James walked back behind the van and quietly talked to each of the deputies and made sure they were all properly suited up. He had made all of them wear their face shields.

12 Pursuit

Alex checked everyone on her team and made sure they were ready. She again told them that the two they were going to apprehend were dangerous. If possible, they would go in quietly and catch the two asleep.

The entire group walked slowly and quietly toward the house. James waited until his deputies were in position.

He led the way to the house. They walked around to the back. There was a single light on in the kitchen.

Alex walked to the kitchen door and used a thin flat flexible metal blade to slide into door crack and into the bolt area. She was able to push the door quietly open. She signaled for James to enter and followed him through the dining room into the living room area.

Jerry was sleeping on the couch. She crossed in front of James and put her gun to Jerry forehead and one hand on his mouth. She saw the look of surprise as she whispered for him to be silent.

He nodded in agreement.

James and Trey rolled him over and wire tied his hands and feet. Trey put a wide strip of tape over Jerry's mouth and checked to see that he was breathing through his nose. James pointed to his two deputies and indicated that Jerry was in their care.

Alex was pleased to see that Abi had her gun aimed at the steps in a ready to respond position.

The Girl on the Grill

James led the way slowly and quietly up the stairs. Alex counted three rooms. She saw that two had the doors slightly open and the third one was closed. She pointed to the third door and took the lead. She again used the flat flexible blade to slide into the door handle area and quietly pushed the door open.

In one swift movement she pushed the door open, took a step in and to the left. James followed and took a step to the right. Alex immediately turned on her high-power light beam, yelled police and rushed forward toward the bed.

She was almost overcome by the deafening roar of the shot gun and the immediate smell of gunpowder. She reacted on pure instinct and the rush of adrenalin as she used her light and the barrel of her gun to push the shot gun barrel into the air as a second round fired. Her foot came up and stomped on Denise's chest. The cracking of the bones, the scream of pain and the fact that the shot gun was dropped, as a third round went off and blew a hole in the ceiling above the bed, let her know that she had been effective.

What kind of woman slept with a loaded shot gun was what went through Alex's mind.

The ceiling plaster board fragments rained down and scattered around the room and a layer of white dust made it hard to see clearly.

The lights came on and the scene alarmed Alex. Trey had rolled a screaming Denise over on her stomach as she tried to reach for the gun under her pillow.

12 Pursuit

He had pushed the gun off the bed to the floor. He then used the restraining wire ties and tied her hands behind her back.

Alex knew that the screaming was probably because of the extreme pain that the broken ribs were most likely causing but at the moment she did not care.

The first blast of the shot gun had hit Abi right in the middle of the protective vest and thrown her back into the wall hard enough to have partially caved in the wall. The second shot had gone upward but had grazed James's helmet and knocked it off.

James was untouched and was on his knees checking on Abi. He took off her face shield that had several pellets embedded in it. He then opened her vest. The outside surface of the vest was riddled with pellet holes, but the vest had held, none had made it through.

Alex was sure Abi would have a huge bruise, but she would live.

James put his ear to Abi's chest and then gave three chest compressions followed by a breath of air. He repeated the process three times before Abi groaned and asked what had happened.

Alex let out her breath. She had not known she had stopped breathing. She was relieved when Abi began to talk.

Alex told Trey to take off the wire ties on Denise's hands and put them to the front. She asked James to call in the rescue support from the Stone County Hospital.

Even in pain, Denise was cursing and fighting Trey.

The Girl on the Grill

The two deputies in the living room came rushing in with their guns drawn. One of them said thank God. Both of them came toward the bed with their guns aimed at Denise.

Alex asked Trey to check on Jerry to make sure he was still breathing and told him to take the tape off of his mouth.

She then went over to Abi and asked her how she felt.

Abi looked at her and replied that she felt like the proverbial mule had kicked her. She went on to quip that others in the department had warned her that it was dangerous to be around Alex and now she knew why.

Alex agreed that it seemed she kept attracting the kind of attention she worked hard to avoid.

Alex looked at James and asked him to bring his car and park it in the driveway with his lights flashing.

She held Ali's hand and sat down on the floor beside her.

She told a yelling Denise that if she didn't shut up, she would come over and stomp on her other ribs.

Alex closed her eyes and went over the entrance to the room and what she should have done differently. Absentmindedly she picked up James's helmet and examined the six pellets that were lodged in the face shield and helmet. She was glad that her presence had caused him to suit up in full gear.

She picked up Abi's face shield. She showed both of the face shields to Abi.

12 Pursuit

Abi touched each embedded pellet with fingers. She thanked Alex for insisting on the full body armor and the face shields. She commented that she was sure James would also thank her.

There was nothing to do but wait. Alex prioritized who she wanted treated by the EMT's. Then she thought about the back up support they needed to bring in. Denise would need to be treated and allowed to mend enough to travel back to Cincinnati. This meant that an around the clock police presence would be needed. Abi would need to be checked out and watched for a couple of days. James needed to be checked out as well, but he seemed to be untouched. She and Trey would stay in Wiggins until it was time to move Denise.

When James came back in, he seemed to read her mind and told her that he would assign an around the clock watch of Denise. She would be hand cuffed to her hospital bed.

The arrival of the EMT was swift. Their appraisal of the situation and decision to take both Denise and Abi to the hospital at the same time was a relief to Alex. She listened as they called in the situation.

She followed them out as they took the two stretchers to the ambulance. One of the deputies was guiding Jerry out to the back of his car. He told Alex that he was taking him to the one cell that they had back in the office.

Alex asked Trey to take their van and to follow James and then bring him to the hospital for a checkup.

The Girl on the Grill

The sun was just making its appearance over the horizon when Alex climbed into the back of the ambulance.

She was looking at the two women on the stretchers. They were both covered with a blanket. Abi had her eyes closed and was breathing easily. The EMT's said they had given her a relaxant so that she would be comfortable.

Denise had her eyes open and when she saw that Alex was at her feet, she tried to kick. She told Alex what a sorry bitch she was and that she wished that the rocket that she had launched would have found Alex in the apartment.

The EMT in charge of monitoring the two patients was sitting directly in front of Alex. He was constantly looking at his equipment monitors and then he would look back at her.

Alex ignored the constant stream of curses and the crying about her having killed Bradley that was coming from Denise. Denise had gotten the same relaxant that Abi had received but it seemed to only make her more active.

Alex found it harder to ignore the EMT. His stare was actually making her nervous.

Once at the hospital she decided to call the Chief to see about getting some help in handling the situation she found herself in.

The first thing she said when he picked up the phone was that she had apprehended both suspects. Then she followed with a description of what had happened and the situation as it stood.

She could see the Chief run his hand across his bald head as he took in the situation.

12 Pursuit

The Chief asked her to have James call him when he got to the hospital. He told Alex that he could have the needed support down to Wiggins by that evening as long as there was no objection by James.

He emphasized that he wanted to make sure Abi got good care and that he wanted a detailed report with on the scene pictures. He said he would send down the site processing crew to document the scene of the crime.

Alex replied that she appreciated his support, and he would get the report he desired.

When she got off the phone, she was again surprised by the EMT that had ridden in the back of the ambulance with her. He introduced himself as Mathew and a life-long friend of James. He explained that they had served in the same army unit together.

He asked if she wanted some coffee and maybe a light breakfast.

Alex appraised the rather tall, slender but clearly very well-conditioned Black man making the offer. His green sparkling eyes captured her. It was the one feature that made her wonder about his family tree. She figured he was about her age. She felt rather good about being hit on and decided against her normal, no thank-you response and instead she said thank-you and that coffee, and some breakfast would help her.

She accepted on the condition that she buy breakfast. She was pleased to hear his response that breakfast couldn't get much better.

The Girl on the Grill

She was listening to Mathew as he told of his friendship with James. They had gone to school together since grade school. They had both been on the same high school football team. He was the receiver and James the quarterback. They had attended West Point and then each got assigned to a unit where they had their own platoon. In Afghanistan they had taken turns saving each other. That experience had bonded them as brothers. He had taken the EMT job so that he could be in the same location as James.

Alex was surprised at her reaction. She was really into what Mathew was saying and missed the hush in the cafeteria until it was too late.

Denise was still handcuffed to her bed rail but had somehow managed to get loose and then overpower the deputy standing outside the door of the hospital room. She had walked up from the side and was about to use the bed rail like a sword to hit Mathew on the back of the head.

In a totally reflex movement, Alex pushed the table with all her strength and Mathew fell over backwards. The bed rail swing missed Mathew but caught Alex on the chest and knocked her to the floor.

Denise let out a cackle and swung the bed rail downward toward Alex.

Alex kicked the side of Denise's leg as hard as she could. The kick was effective in knocking Denise off balance and the swinging bedrail hit the floor next to Alex's right side.

12 Pursuit

Alex jumped up and hit Denise with a chop to the side of her neck and followed with a finger jab to her eyes.

Screaming that she had been blinded, Denise fell to her knees with her hands over her eyes.

The deputy posted outside of her hospital room had recovered and had come in just as Alex pushed Denise to the floor. He took over and put handcuffs on her wristed.

Mathew was still sitting on the floor trying to figure out what had happened when Alex came over and asked if he was alright.

When Alex took Mathew's hand to help him up, she felt a shiver go up her back. He looked at her and his green eyes seemed to look deep within her. She felt like he was looking at her soul. It was a feeling that she had never experienced.

When Mathew pulled her toward him, she at first thought he was making an advance, but the sound of a gun kicked her into automatic.

She pushed Mathew as hard as she could as she pulled her gun and went down on one knee as she spun around.

Denise had somehow taken the deputies gun and with her hands still handcuffed together she was using both hands to manipulate the gun. She was never able to finish pulling the trigger for the second shot because Alex had put two bullets into her chest.

Denise fell to her knees and was trying to raise her gun for a shot when Alex's third shot hit her between the eyes. Denise was cursing at Alex as she fell face down, flat to the floor.

The Girl on the Grill

Alex rose and stepped forward and moved the gun Denise had used and checked for a pulse. There was none. This time the bullet had not come out the back of the head.

She stopped the deputy from picking up his gun and told him to step back. His gun was evidence. She told him to close the cafeteria and to tape off the scene. She had put her gun down on a nearby table. She was taking pictures while she waited for the sheriff's office to send over a team to work the scene.

Mathew cautiously approached Alex and asked her if she knew she was bleeding.

Once again, his green eyes seemed to stop her brain. She asked what he was talking about.

He waved over to the nurse who had come with the gurney to transport Denise and asked her to bring him a first aid kit. He pulled over a chair and asked Alex to sit down. Once Alex was sitting, she felt Mathew's left hand push her hair up on the back of her head.

She heard Mathew take a short breath in as he saw her neck.

He described it as a shallow grove across the back of her neck and on the top of her left shoulder. It would need to be closed. He sprayed on a numbing agent.

Alex had not felt the burning sensation until he mentioned its location. It had not registered during her adrenaline high but now it was making it presence known.

12 Pursuit

Mathew sprayed on a disinfectant. Then he sprayed on a clear sealer as he held the grove closed. He was able to almost make the grove invisible. He hoped that the scar would be so thin that it would be almost invisible.

Alex relaxed and followed the movement of Mathew's hands. He was professional and explained each step of the treatment.

A hospital doctor had come in but had stood back until Mathew was done. He then took a quick look at the wound and complimented Mathew on the excellent work. He looked into Alex's eyes, tested her eye movement, and went on to listen to her heart and breathing. He asked how she felt and whether she needed any counseling.

Alex thanked him and told him that she felt fine and was it OK to continue to take her pictures.

She stood up and asked Mathew what he liked to be called.

He smiled and said that Matt was what he was called by all his friends.

She asked him if he was alright after having been so rudely pushed and landing on his butt.

He smiled and said that she could save him anytime she desired.

13 Mississippi

The county coroner came in and took control of the scene. After a round of picture taking and checking Denise's body, he signaled his two associates to put Denise into a body bag and take the body to the mortuary. He would do an autopsy in the morning.

The hospital bed handrail was still on the floor next to the turned over table and the fallen chair. Two deputies were taking pictures, talking with Alex and Mathew, and recording their statements.

Mathew thanked Alex for saving him from having his head bashed in and for the free breakfast. She in turn thanked him for the great first aid treatment.

James came and asked what had happened. Alex listened to Mathew's account of what had happened. She was surprised at how precise Mathew's description was and how much credit he gave her for her cool selfless actions.

13 Mississippi

Trey had been standing nearby and listening. He teased Alex about becoming Cincinnati's Annie Oakley. Mathew added that he had never seen anyone so steady in shooting when being shot at.

James made a comment that the two of them would have valued a platoon member with her skills when they were fighting in Afghanistan.

Mathew acted surprised and comment that he did not think of Afghanistan at all but about the cafeteria scene and being saved from a mad woman with a gun.

Alex thanked them but said that she had hit her first two shots by accident and the third one was because her finger was shaking so much that the gun just went off.

She was actually feeling good about their comments, but she felt a little embarrassed. She had no doubt that the Chief's constant push for all of them to practice their shooting had once again paid off.

Trey went on that from now on he was not going to let her go off alone with some unknown guy for breakfast by her lonesome.

He teased Alex about becoming "Cincinnati's Black Annie Oakley.

The Girl on the Grill

Alex spoke up and made it clear that it had been Mathew that had saved her life when he pulled her into his arms. She was happy to see the surprised look on Mathew's face and amused about his reply that it was the first time in his life that a woman had reacted so negatively to his come on and pushed him away with so much force that he had landed on his butt.

Alex replied that the next time they had breakfast it would be in Cincinnati, and it again would be her treat.

She excused herself and left the cafeteria. Her first stop was the bathroom. Then she placed a call to the Chief. She knew she would once again face a two-week mandatory suspension while she was cleared by internal affairs. She had already placed her weapon into an evidence bag. By the time she got all the reports done and had talked to the councilors half her suspension time would be done.

The Chief listened to her account and told her to take her time. He would cancel the folks that he had been planning to send down and he would arrange for the transport of Jerry back to Cincinnati. She, Trey, and Abi were to drive back in the next few days.

The conversation with the chief reminded Alex she should go and check in on Abi. She went from the lobby to Abi's room.

Abi had been dosing and enjoying the comfort of her bed. The relaxant that Mathew had given her was wearing off and she was starting to feel the dull throbbing pain associated with the impact of a shot gun blast at such a close range.

13 Mississippi

Alex took in Abi's smile and listened to Abi thank her for making them all wear their full assault gear. She commented that she was not sure her regular vest would have saved her. She had learned that her heart had stopped but that James's quick resuscitation efforts had saved her.

Alex told Abi about what had just happened in the cafeteria and that Denise was dead.

Abi said that it was great news. She said that she would have hated to spend time getting ready to go to court and to watch the bitch try to manipulate the system.

Alex told her the Chief had said to take their time until she was released and ready to travel.

She was surprised to hear Abi say she was planning to take all her vacation time and stay in Wiggins. She commented that there was a handsome sheriff she was going to get to know better. If it worked out, she might stay in Wiggins for a long time more.

Alex called Trey and asked him where he was at the moment. He responded that he was still in the cafeteria. The scene had been completely examined and photographed, and the cleaning crew had just arrived.

She asked Trey to arrange for them to get a ride back to their van.

They were taken back to their van. After putting all their gear into the storage lockers, they drove up to Denise's house. The deputy that had brought them to their van was standing and talking to another deputy that apparently was standing guard of the house.

The Girl on the Grill

Alex got out of the van and thanked both deputies for doing a great job. She gave them a standing invitation to lunch if they ever got to Cincinnati.

She cringed when one of them replied that it would be an honor to have lunch with Cincinnati's Annie Oakley.

Once back in the van, Trey said he would try to keep her new moniker quiet when they returned to Cincinnati.

Alex thanked him and said that she was looking forward to getting back to Cincinnati and perhaps enjoying a few dull weeks of routine work.

After a brief discussion she and Trey decided that they would return to Cincinnati the following day. Trey said he was not surprised about Abi's decision to stay.

They asked James if they were allowed to transport Jerry back. James suggested that they not do so because both of them had been part of the assault on the house and Alex had subsequently shot and killed the second person that was on the extradition paperwork. He said he had talked with her Chief and agreed that a transport team would be sent to pick Jerry up once everything was cleared up.

Alex felt a sense of relief. She and Trey would be able to relax on their trip back.

13 Mississippi

Back in Cincinnati, Alex found out that the drug distribution raid was successful. Bill and Travis had made little headway in tracking down Ralph Donaldson the local drug distributor and apparent initial love interest of Mandy Millwright, the girl on the grill.

The DEA had been successful in tracking the trucks to the east coast distribution locations and in subsequent raids had severely disrupted the distribution. Everyone was pleased with the success but had no illusions about the continued flow of the drugs. They knew some other group would step in to fill the pull of the needy customers.

Alex contacted Johnnie and asked how he liked his new job. He said it was great to have a place to call home and did she have time for lunch.

Johnnie began by saying that he had known she was home but had refrained from calling on her. He figured she would contact him when she was ready.

Alex thanked him for being considerate. She asked him if he had done any more investigation into the girl on the grill case. She was happy to learn that he had done so.

Johnnie had learned that Mandy had regularly been seen with Ralph at several bars and night clubs. Johnnie had gone to each and either had a beer or a lunch and talked with the bar tender or a waiter.

The Girl on the Grill

He learned that Ralph was always showing Mandy off as his prized girl. She always played the part of a willing lover. She was at his table most of the times when it seemed to the observers that business was being negotiated.

Alex asked Johnnie to submit a formal report and to include the expenses he had incurred doing the research. The expenses were to include office space, transportation, meals, and drinks. His time was to be the standard expert consulting expense that had been agreed to by HR.

Alex shared Johnnie's report with the Chief. He in turn called in Bill, Travis, and Trey into his office to share the report and to reinvigorate the search for Ralph. He asked Bill and Travis to go to each location mentioned in the report and dig a little deeper.

He wanted Ralph apprehended and brought in as an accomplice to murder. The DEA wanted him on drug distribution charges but had agreed that a murder charge would be better than what they had on him. They figured if the murder charge failed, they would follow up with the drug distribution charge.

After the meeting, the chief asked Alex and Trey to remain. He let them know that he had nominated them for public recognition of their bravery in the line of duty.

Trey commented that he certainly recognized Alex's right to such an honor but that he had just been along for most of it.

The Chief asked if he had rushed into a room where shotguns were being fired or had he run the other way?

13 Mississippi

Alex commented that she was able to rush in because she knew Trey had her back and he should be quiet and accept the award with a thank-you.

The Chief nodded and waved them from his office.

Bill asked if the Chief had just told them about the award.

Alex looked around the bull pen. She asked if she and Trey were the only ones that had been clueless?

Bill responded that everyone had learned about it as soon as the Chief had put in his recommendation. He went on to say that everyone agreed, and everyone, including he and Travis were in support.

Alex thanked him for letting her know. She looked around the bull pen and thanked everyone. She was shocked when from almost every desk a sign went up. Everyone had some version of Alex Evercrest, the Cincinnati Annie Oakley.

She was even more surprised when the Chief came out of his office with his Annie Oakley sign and put his thumb pointing up.

She had tears in her eyes as she told Trey that she was going for a drive and would he like to come along.

Once in the car she looked over to Trey.

She smiled at him and told him that as penance for starting the Annie Oakley comparison, his family picnic this coming weekend had better consist of grilled asparagus, scallops, steak, and a big buttered baked potato.

Trey looked at her and joked that she was going to drive him to drink.

The Girl on the Grill

They both belonged to the same AA group, and this had become their common reply when they had nothing better to say.

After a short trip down to the waterfront, she returned to the station. She entered and went to her locker and changed out of her office attire.

She went out to her bike that the shop had delivered to her apartment. An accompanying note clarified that there was no charge. She unlocked the bile and headed for her apartment.

She followed about the same routine each day. She took a slightly different route to and from the office each day. She did her workout in the evening at various times and periodically did them in the morning. She had decided that she should not be too predictable.

She stopped by Johnnie's apartment to thank him for having done such a great job on his investigation and on the reports he had written. She told him that Bill and Travis were going to do a detailed follow-up.

She then went up to her apartment.

The following day she took an Uber to Trey's home in Montgomery.

Lindsey greeted Alex and thanked her for coming over for the family grill out. Alex and Lindsey had become very good friends. Nolan called her Aunt Alex.

Alex had brought two bottles of her favorite Muscat alcohol free wine as her contribution to the meal.

13 Mississippi

Alex enjoyed playing with Nolan and reading him a book of his choice. His favorite was the Taelo series by Ron Mueller about a young boy growing up in ancient times.

Trey was out at the grill, but Lindsey said that they were eating inside where they could all avoid the heat and humidity.

Alex chuckled when Trey brought in the grill asparagus, steak and scallops and pointed at each. Lindsey took out the baked potato prepared with butter and cheese with a sprinkle of dried onions over the top.

That is when Nolan carried in a sign saying, Alex, Our Annie Oakley.

Alex got down on her knees and gave him a hug as she looked over his shoulders at Trey and Lindsey holding each other and sporting beaming smiles.

She had tears of joy in her eyes. It was great to have such good friends.

Lindsey then took a series of pictures before getting everyone seated.

Alex stayed until it was Nolan's bedtime.

She had gone out to the Montgomery area in an Uber but returned in a Lyft. She figured she would spread her support for the businesses out.

She sent a tip to the driver from her app and got out in front of her apartment. After entering her tenants code, she went in and pushed the button to the elevator.

The Girl on the Grill

Once in her apartment she did her yoga and her Tae-Chi exercises. Then it was a quick shower. She was ready for bed.

Monday made it two weeks, and her suspension was up. She would still need to requalify her gun skills.

Her first action was to go and get her recertification. The gun master welcomed her and gave her fresh ammunition for her gun. He checked her gun, had her put on her safety glasses and hearing protection.

She turned, raised her gun, and slowly but steadily emptied her gun into three spots on the target, two to the head, two to each side of the breastbone. She had discharged her gun in a clockwise rotation. First to the heart, second to the right of the breastbone and third to the forehead. She had then repeated the cycle. It had taken her less than thirty seconds.

She laughed when the target was pulled in and the gun master said that she had either put each second shot into the same hole, or she had missed with three shots.

She told him to look at the tracking cameras and tell her how good she was.

He played the tracking video and just whistled and said he now understood the comment about her being Cincinnati's black female Annie Oakley detective.

He asked if she wanted a paper copy of her certificate. She replied that the email copy would be sufficient.

13 Mississippi

She went back to her desk and put on her shoulder holster, sat down, and cleaned her gun and then put in the bullets and put the gun into its holster.

She straightened out her jacket and hunched her shoulders. It had been two weeks since she felt fully dressed.

Trey commented that she looked good and that he could now relax since he was protected by the best.

She smiled at the compliment and suggested they find out what Bill and Travis had found out.

Trey called Travis and agreed to meet for lunch at one of the local bars that was on the investigate list.

Alex agreed that would be a good place to catch up.

Bill and Travis had not learned much more than Johnnie. The description about Ralph's public display of his sexual dominance of Mandy was more graphic than the one Johnnie had been given.

It was clear that Ralph treated her as a possession to display. He also seemed to offer her to some of his clients.

Alex asked if Bill and Travis had sensed anyone that might be holding back any information. Travis replied that out of the six places they had visited there was only one place. That was the bar across from the drug house where it seemed all the local action took place.

Alex said that she would go to that bar and see what she could stir up. Travis and Bill said to go for it but to be careful. They both commented that the bar was definitely a hangout for white supremacists as well as druggies.

The Girl on the Grill

Alex thanked them and told them that she would let them know if she found out anything.

She went to her car and she and Trey drove to the West side bar.

After parking, Alex took off the strap holding her gun and got out. After warning Trey not to react to any name calling, she followed him into the dimly lit bar. It was tidy and seemed to be well kept.

Trey introduced them as police detectives following up on the previous visit by two other officers from the department.

The bar tender said that he recalled the earlier two and asked what Trey wanted. He seemed to be ignoring Alex.

One of three burley men sitting at the bar, with blue hard hats at their feet made a loud comment about a Whitey coming in with a Black bitch at his heals and was she his dog.

Alex took in the three but gave no response. She noted that Trey continued to focus on talking to the bartender.

She was surprised when one of the three got up out of his seat and bully walked toward them.

She took a step forward to place herself in between the on comer and Trey.

She held up her badge and clearly stated that she was a police officer.

The bully loudly replied that he didn't care what kind of Black trash she might be.

13 Mississippi

Alex was surprised when the on comer raised his fist to strike her. She waited until the swing was on its way then she took a smooth flowing step to the side and her right flat hand guided the fist, past her face.

She then stiffened her fingers of the same hand and struck the attacker in the eyes and quickly followed with a strike to his throat.

As he fell to his knees Trey pulled his hands behind his back and cuffed him and pushed him the rest of the way to the floor.

Alex shifted her attention to the two at the bar as they stood up. She told them to sit back down and finish their drink.

With her eyes on them and a quick glance at the bartender she called for backup.

It took less than two minutes for the backup to arrive. She told the backup to take the attacker in and book him for assaulting a police officer. She listened as one of the backups recited the Miranda to the coughing arrestee.

She asked Trey if he was done with the bartender. Trey replied the he had just gotten started. He turned back to the bartender. Alex relaxed when the two backups returned and stood just inside the door.

One of the two remaining workers at the bar asked if they could leave.

Alex replied they were free to leave. Alex turned to one of the backup officers and asked that the two be escorted out and watched to make sure they left the parking lot.

The Girl on the Grill

Two more back up officers arrived and the original two let her know they were taking their prisoner to booking.

Alex took their names and badge number and asked them to make a clean report. She would add her details when she returned to the station.

Trey thanked the bartender, turned to Alex, and told her that he had gotten an address that the bartender had gotten from a check.

Alex called Bill and gave him the address. She replied sure, your welcome and that she and Trey would meet them at the address.

Alex drove to within a block of the address and waited for Bill and Travis to arrive. She got out her and Trey's bullet proof vests.

She commented that she preferred a full body suit for these occasions. She and Trey got back into the car to wait.

She saw Bill approaching from behind. She waved them on and then followed as they drove into the driveway. She parked in the street in front of the house.

Bill waved them to the front and indicated he and Travis were going around back.

Alex had just stepped to the side of the front door when she heard two gunshots from the back of the house.

She ran back down the steps and almost ran into Bill. He and Travis were going after a person who had run out and jumped the fence. They had heard a car start and take off. He told her to go around the block ahead of her. They would go the other way. She could hear Travis as he called in for backup support.

13 Mississippi

Alex took off and went around and to the right. She went on straight as she looked to the left and Trey looked to the right as they passed each street. They went about six blocks and nothing unusual was happening. She came to a stop light and pulled into an empty lot.

Trey called Travis and learned that whoever had been in the house had escaped. They had obtained permission to enter the house and were just getting to the driveway. Travis let them know they had a backup unit with them.

Alex turned her car and proceeded back to the house.

This time she parked across the street. She and Trey entered the house and were met by the two backups.

Trey asked Bill if they had found anything. Bill held up a picture of Mandy being held by Ralph. Travis held up a black book and commented that it had some names and addresses.

Alex congratulated them on a successful bust but that now all they had to do was to catch Ralph. Bill held up a descriptive finger and said thanks and that he loved her too. Alex replied that she and Trey were headed back to the office to finish the day. They had a prisoner to process and then a report to write.

Alex was right in how long it was going to take to process the prisoner.

She also had no clue the direction the case was going to take.

14 Cincinnati's Annie Oakley

Processing the barroom attacker and writing the report took longer than Alex would have liked but she wanted it done before she quit for the day. She had Trey, who had a family life, go home at the end of the regular workday. It took her another hour before she was in the locker room changing into her biking outfit. She was looking forward to getting back to her apartment and then working out for an hour. She figured she would have a snack after her workout.

She rode the elevator to the sixth floor and walked to the end of the hallway to her apartment. She let go of her bike and held with her hip as she put the key into the bolt lock to open the door. She put her key back into her bag and opened the door with her left hand and pushed her bike into the room with her right hand.

Alex knew immediately something was wrong. The kitchen lights were off. She dropped the bike and was reaching for her weapon when a voice told to pick up the bike or he would shoot.

14 Cincinnati's Annie Oakley

Alex was surprised to see Ralph Donaldson step from the small alcove leading to the guest bedroom and bathroom. She asked if she could put her bike out on the porch. Ralph stepped to the back of the living room and waved his gun to indicate she should go ahead. Alex noted that the glass on the door had been broken. She figured that Ralph had come in through the porch.

She asked Ralph how he had managed to get to her porch. He laughed and told her that he went to the fourth floor where they were doing the repair work on her old apartment and climbed the two levels using the corner pole and handrails. He went on to say it was an easy climbing for anyone, but he actually climbed cliffs for sport. He had originally planned to climb up from the ground.

Ralph asked Alex to put her gun on the middle of the dining table and then go stand in front of the stove.

Alex was just going to ask what Ralph had in mind when the doorbell rang. She was not expecting anyone and was surprised.

Ralph asked if she were expecting anyone and she replied she had no clue who might be at the door. She went on to say that it was probably some salesman or some person trying to save her soul.

Ralph chuckled and told her to get rid of whoever it was.

Alex almost froze when she cracked the door and looked into beautiful green eyes. She immediately said she was not interested and asked how a salesman had gotten into the building. She went on to say "go away and get a friend to buy your junk. Then she slammed the door shut.

The Girl on the Grill

Ralph asked if she were always so sharp.

Alex said no she normally listened to their sales line, but she normally did not have a gun aimed at her back.

Ralph agreed it was a wise move. He waved her back to the place he wanted her.

Alex was not sure how Mathew had gotten into the building, but he had been holding flowers and a bottle. She was certain that Mathew would get the idea that something was wrong. She planned to stall and hope that help arrived in time.

She turned to Ralph and asked what he had in mind.

Ralph replied that maybe he had come on a romantic call and would just enjoy having her.

Alex smiled and unbuttoned the top two buttons of her shirt. Then she calmly told Ralph that if he got that close, he would die.

Ralph opened his eyes as if surprised and mentioned that he was the one with the gun.

Alex was both flirting and baiting Ralph. She wanted to give the police time to respond.

Outside her door, Mathew's initial reaction was a kind of rejection shock then it hit him that something was very wrong.

He had somehow gotten Johnnie's number and had called Johnnie to let him into the building. Mathew first called 911 and reported a home break in and gave the address and the residents name.

He then called Johnnie and told him about his exchange with Alex. Johnnie said he was going to call in the cavalry.

14 Cincinnati's Annie Oakley

Johnnie called the Chief at home. A surprised Chief was going to ask how Johnnie had his home number, but Johnnie blurted out that Alex was in trouble. She needed help.

The Chief said he would get a team out to help. He in turn called the night desk and told them to get a swat team out to Alex's apartment. He told them not to use any sirens or lights.

Everything was in motion. It had taken less than three minutes for help to be on the way.

Alex was clueless as to what was going on outside. She knew that her survival was probably in her hands. Ralph was hers to apprehend or to take out, but external distraction would be helpful.

She asked again what he had in mind.

Ralph said he was taking her hostage, and she would drive him to Missouri in her car.

She asked what was in Missouri for him to go to.

His response was that it was none of her business.

Alex agreed she would do it and asked what would happen when they got to Missouri. She had no intention of complying, but she was stalling for time. She added that by that time the two of them might even get to like each other.

The swat team was in place in less than nine minutes. A sniper was on top of the building across from the parking garage. One window offered a clear view of the interior of the apartment. Unfortunately, Ralph was standing in front of the window with the blinds pulled closed.

The Girl on the Grill

Alex saw the red light of the laser and knew Mathew had reported the situation. It was time for her to act.

She began by stating that Ralph was actually rather handsome and perhaps they could work something out.

She took a couple of steps toward Ralph and watched as a smile or perhaps it was a smirk come to his face. He was just about to reply when the apartment door seemed to explode and fly into the room.

Ralph had taken a step back and was now against the window.

Alex moved immediately and threw herself into a long flying tackle. The shot from Ralph's gun missed her and later it would be found lodged in the side of the refrigerator that until her dive had been directly behind her.

She took a forward roll over the coffee table and with her left hand she knocked the gun from Ralph's hand. She hit his Adam's Apple with the stiff fingers of her right hand.

She was about to hit him again in the throat when she was pulled back by a swat team member. Ralph fell to the floor and was gagging. The medic called for the respirator. A third medic came in and put the tube down Ralph's throat.

The last Alex took in was Ralph's rasping and trying breathing.

She suddenly realized that the person guiding her down the hallway was Mathew. She looked into his eyes, said thank-you, and gave him a kiss.

14 Cincinnati's Annie Oakley

The green eyes had previously captured her mind; the electricity of the kiss burned her soul. This she knew was the person that she was looking for.

Mathew smiled and said he was hoping for the connection, and he had brought flowers and wine, but he was not sure he could keep up with someone who was constantly being shot at or being bombed.

Alex was still in shock about the entire episode. She wanted a quiet place to sit and relax.

Johnnie had watched the crashing in of the door, Alex being escorted out and then, what he thought of as, the love scene in the hallway.

He approached the two and took the flowers and the bottles of wine and told Mathew and Alex to follow him. He led the way down to his apartment.

He was proud to show Alex the new décor and the paints on the wall. They were real paintings he had purchased from an artist friend.

Alex sat down at the table accepted a glass of wine when she found out that it was alcohol free. She looked at Mathew and complimented him on his choice of wine. She took note that he had learned the simple fact about her needing to be alcohol free.

She was next surprised when there was a knock on the door. Johnnie opened the door, and the Chief and Trey walked in.

The Chief walked in and looked around. He complimented Johnnie on the paintings and asked where he had purchased them.

The Girl on the Grill

Johnnie looked over at Alex and beamed a smile.

Then the Chief looked at Johnnie and asked how he had gotten his home number.

Johnnie replied that it was in the computer under the departments phone list. He went to the refrigerator and pointed to the Chief's name and number. He commented that it had come in pretty handy.

The Chief laughed and told Johnnie he wanted to have a copy of the list to put on his refrigerator at his house.

Alex recounted how Ralph had used the porch corner pole on the building to get to her apartment. She asked Johnnie to figure out a way to make it harder for people to climb up the building. She also asked that her porch door be replaced with one that was solid steel similar to her front apartment door that also needed replacing. She commented that she hoped the building had a good super.

The aroma from the oven caused her to ask what Johnnie was cooking. He responded that he had put a large pepperoni and cheese pizza into the oven as a snack.

The Chief and Trey both declined the pizza and said it was time to go home.

Alex, Mathew, and Johnnie sat at the table and enjoyed a large helping of pizza.

Johnnie said he would take a large piece of plywood up and arrange for a temporary way to close the door opening.

14 Cincinnati's Annie Oakley

Alex took the bouquet of flowers and Mathew's hand and led the way to the elevators.

Once Johnnie had the plywood in place and Mathew had screwed it in place from the inside, Alex poured a glass of wine and once again asked Mathew what he was doing in Cincinnati.

He replied that he had learned the Annie Oakley of Cincinnati was single and available.

He let her know that he had quit his job in Wiggins and had taken one in Cincinnati so he could make his move.

Alex took another sip of her wine, stood up, took his hand, and asked if he was interested in a shower.

The End

Preview of: Missing

Preview of: Missing

Missing

1 Cold Case by a Hand from Above

*A*lex and Trey, her detective partner were back in Cincinnati after pursuing a lunatic person in Mississippi. This person had destroyed Alex's apartment with a rocket propelled grenade. They had almost been shot by this person with a shotgun during her apprehension and later at the local hospital this same woman managed to escape from her hospital bed, take a policeman's gun, and shoot at Alex. Alex's swift reflex and deadly aim ended the confrontation with the woman face down on the floor from a shot to the chest and one between her eyes.

During that case, Alex had survived two attacks in her own Cincinnati apartment.

The first was the rocket propelled grenade, launched by the lunatic that Alex had ultimately killed in Mississippi, had demolished her first apartment.

Preview of: Missing

The second attack was on her return from Mississippi. The drug distributor involved in the case had gained access to her new apartment by climbing externally up two floors to her exterior apartment porch.

She had picked up a suitor in Mississippi that had followed her to Cincinnati. He was the EMT that she had met in Mississippi. His unexpected knock on her apartment door, when she was being held at gun point, had given her the opportunity to get help.

She had told him to go away and that solicitors were not allowed in the building. He had figured out that something was wrong. He called the Cincinnati Chief of police and asked for help. When help arrived and was breaking down the door, Alex dived at the intruder as he shot at her. In the ensuing struggle the intruder was shot by his own gun. He survived.

She had shot and killed two people in less than a month. Her swift actions and her swift and deadly shooting had earned her the handle of "the Cincinnati's Black Annie Oakley."

Alex leaned back in her chair and took in the few detectives that were currently sitting at their desks.

She and Trey were both stressed out.

He had moved to Cincinnati to get away from the stress of a similar situation during his tenure as a policeman in Milwaukee. Before taking a job in the Milwaukee police department, he had survived Afghanistan. He knew he had a case of PTSD, and he was also enrolled in Alcoholics Anonymous with Alex.

Preview of: Missing

Trey recognized that he was now partnered at work with a person that seemed to be a magnet for violence but who had gotten him help with his dependence on alcohol, who had become a close family friend and who was adored by his son, Nolan.

He knew he would have a lifetime of managing the stress, but he had a work partner that he could look to for help, an adoring beautiful wife, and a son to greet him after each day's work.

A few days after their return from Mississippi, Johnnie, the old Vietnam veteran that Alex had recruited to work for her, and the police department had surprised both of them by coming into the office. He was excited and said he had the perfect case for them to handle. He was sure Alex could solve a long-standing cold case about a missing girl. He had gotten interested in her when the local news had highlighted the fifteenth anniversary of her disappearance. He had used his investigative skills on his personal computer and on the office police computer. He was sure he had some new leads for Alex to follow.

Alex thanked him and slowly reviewed his report. As always, Johnnie had a solid, thorough in-depth report. It was clear this case had somehow caught his interest because he had done an analysis of every individual mentioned in the original police report. The mother and father of the missing child still lived in Cincinnati Area.

Preview of: Missing

The mother worked at a major food store. The father was a truck driver. They had two additional children ages nine and seven. It sounded like a case she might someday look into. She again thanked Johnnie but said she was not ready to dig into the case at the moment.

Johnnie let out a small groan and looked disappointed, but he said he would wait until she was ready. Then he would help her in any way possible. He got up and said he would see the two of them later.

Alex and Trey had been promised a couple of easy weeks by the Cincinnati's Chief of detectives, Bruce Johnson, and he had delivered but he was now beckoning the two of them into his office.

Oh no, escaped from her mouth as she stood up.

Trey had heard her exclamation and just said Ditto.

The Chief's office door leading to the detective work area had been left open and Alex followed by Trey walked slowly toward it in an apprehensive way. The hair on the back of her neck had automatically stood up when the Chief signaled to them. She hoped that he remembered that he had promised to go easy on the two of them for a few weeks.

As she and Trey walked in, Alex looked at the chief and then took in the mild-mannered woman with black hair sitting stiffly upright in the chair in front of the chief's desk. The woman seemed nervous. Alex noted that the woman's her right hand kept clenching her left hand.

Preview of: Missing

Alex let Trey go past her then closed the door. She took in the scene and noted Bruce's nod for her to sit down.

The Chief introduced the woman as Martha Melville a librarian in the Cincinnati Library. He wanted Alex to listen to the story that Martha had to tell.

Alex asked if Martha happened to know Johnnie Lancaster. Martha smiled and said that if he was a black Vietnam veteran that constantly frequented the library and managed to get a few cookies from attending various presentation, then she knew Johnnie.

Alex shared that she had hired him as a computer analyst and had gotten him a job as a super for her apartment building.

Martha smiled and said that explained why she had seen less of Johnnie.

Alex noted that this simple interchange had changed the atmosphere in the room. Martha now seemed to relax as she leaned back in her chair.

The Chief asked Martha to tell her story to Alex and Trey.

Alex listened as Martha recalled the story of Annie Lorie Scots a young girl that had gone missing and had never been found. Martha told of an acquaintance that had told her of a young woman being held in the woods in southern New York state. The timing of the rumors and stories told about the situation seemed to coincide with Annie's disappearance. Martha's informant had not given her the name of the neighbor or the location where Annie might be.

Preview of: Missing

Alex asked for a moment so she could get some information that had been given to her just a few days ago.

Alex walked out and retrieved Johnnie's report. She pulled it from her file and walked back into the office.

Alex asked Martha if she knew anything about Annie's parents.

Martha said she had done a little bit of an investigation on her own. The parents were library members and had two girls that were also members. She said she had written down some of the information that she had dug up.

After rummaging for moment through her purse she pulled out a folded sheet of paper and put it on the desk.

Alex thanked her and leaned forward to read the information on the paper. She was stunned when it matched the one in Johnnie's report.

She thanked Martha and told her that she would be looking into the case. She set up a time that she could speak to Martha at the library.

The Chief escorted Martha out to the front door and thanked her for coming forward. He stood and watched as Martha walked out in the direction of the library.

He was taken aback by the fact that Alex had a quarter inch thick report on a case that he knew nothing about. He then turned and hurried back to his office. He wanted to know how Alex had a report on this specific case.

Preview of: Missing

Alex had relaxed and quietly asked Trey to relax until the Chief came back. She knew he would want to know how she gotten a report on a cold case without his knowledge. She told Trey she would handle the Chief.

The Chief entered his office looked at Alex and asked her to clue him in. He asked how she had gotten the files of a cold case without him knowing it?

Alex explained that it was not an official police cold case file but a report that Johnnie had given her a few days ago. It had been his intention to give her an easy job. He had gotten into the case because of a Cincinnati television station reporting on the fifteenth anniversary on Annie's disappearance.

The Chief took the report and quickly flipped through it. He looked at Alex and asked if she and Trey were ready to get back to work and that he was assigning her to look into and solve the cold case. He said that to him it was no coincident that both Johnnie and Martha the librarian had come forward with the same case. To him it was a biblical sign, and he was going to make an official opening of Annie's cold case.

Alex walked out to the copy machine and made a copy of Johnnie's report. She returned and gave the Chief a copy. She told him to read it slowly and that it would raise the hair on the back of his neck and maybe put some hair on top of his head.

Preview of: Missing

He gruffly told her to get to work. He had confidence that Alex would get to the bottom of the case. He gave a small prayer that she would do it without the fireworks and shootings of the last case.

She gave a salute and walked back to her desk.

She called Johnnie and asked if he would like to sit in as she and Trey developed a plan to look into the case, he had brought to her.

She suggested his apartment as the meeting place if he would provide coffee. The alternative would be the station and station house coffee.

Johnnie chose his apartment and offered to have some donuts or fruit. Alex replied that a banana would do.

She and Trey walked eight blocks to her apartment building where both she and Johnnie lived. She knocked on Johnnie's apartment door and was quickly taken in.

The first thing Johnnie asked was why she had changed her mind about taking up the cold case.

Alex joked with him and told him that she had seen tears in his eyes and had felt so bad that she told Trey they would have to do it.

Johnnie knew immediately that Alex was joking with him and said that he had another tougher case handy if she was interested.

Preview of: Missing

She told Johnnie about Martha's visit to the station and the fact that her information built on the research Johnnie had done. Martha had been the catalyst in getting the cold case recognized but that his research was what opened it.

Johnnie let out a low whistle. He commented that the investigation had an invisible hand guiding it.

Alex smiled and shook her head up and down as she agreed with him. She commented that the Chief had said the same thing when he declared he was opening up Annie's cold case. She commented that a cold shiver had run down her back when she had listened to Martha and it had just done so again. She commented that this was a cold case that she was determined to solve.

She also joked that the Martha had remembered Johnnie as a regular cookie thief.

Johnnie gave a small laugh and confessed that he had scrounged many a cookie by attending presentation session at the Library. It had been a dry, safe, and enjoyable place for him. He said that he would have to bake some cookies and take them to the library as a thank-you gesture.

The plan of how to get into the cold case slowly took shape. Alex asked Johnnie to do some additional on-line searches that might be needed. She and Trey would interview Martha again and go over everything they had to date.

She had identified the person who had closed the case. He was now the sheriff in Loveland. She planned to get him to take a lead role in looking into the case.

Preview of: Missing

They would also see if they could interview the mother and father of the missing girl.

Alex closed the planning session and declared she was going to work out in the Gym. She told Trey to go home early and enjoy the last day of taking it easy.

She suggested they meet the following day at the station. They would begin by setting up appointments with Martha and the Loveland Sheriff.

Johnnie said that he would do the research that Alex had requested.

Alex had a surge of energy that came from the interaction she had with her team. Her team that functioned so smoothly, so efficiently, effectively and was becoming unstoppable. She hoped that they would break the cold case wide open.

Later she would learn that her hopes would be well short of the miracle that awaited but would take her into a lifelong relationship.

Preview of: Missing

2 The Sheriff's Albatross

*A*lex sat in her bed and read over Johnnies' report on Annie. She carefully and thoroughly went through what had happened to Annie. It was 1987 when Annie Scots went out to play with a neighbor. Not much later the neighbor called to ask when Annie was coming over. Annie's mother immediately went out and looked for Annie. She was never found.

For days and weeks, the local news and a few national channels featured the parent's pleas for the return of their daughter. The pleas went unanswered and soon the coverage ended.

The Loveland police department kept the case open for five years. They questioned all neighbors and checked several of them out but had gotten no viable leads.

A yearly plea was still put out by her parents.

Alex got up and Googled Loveland.

In its early days, Loveland was known as a resort town, with its summer homes for the wealthy, earning it the nickname "Little Switzerland of the Miami Valley."

It became known for being extremely safe with a very low crime rate and a family friendly community.

Preview of: Missing

She found the downtown area of Loveland to be charming. It had family-friendly restaurants, a park and the Loveland bike trail that ran from downtown Cincinnati past Loveland for some hundred miles. Alex had ridden through Loveland several times when she went on her long bike rides.

Loveland was about twenty-five miles by car from headquarters.

It can't happen here was erased by Annie's disappearance.

To Alex this incident reinforced her belief that bad things happened in the best communities.

The next morning, as usual she biked to work. Her first stop after changing into her work outfit was the coffee machine. She was greeted by Bill and Travis who were sitting having coffee and a donut. Bill lifted the donut box and offered her one. She thanked him but shook her head to indicate she was passing on the offer.

Trey walked in a few moments later with his coffee in hand. He accepted the offer of a donut.

After a few moments of the four of them chatting, Trey led the way to one of the huddle rooms.

From there she called the Loveland Police office and set up an interview with their Sheriff. Years ago, he was the young deputy that had closed Annie's case. He agreed to an interview but voiced his doubts about having any success in solving the case.

She said that his information and recall was critical, and he might have an insight and know nuances that would not be in a written report. She wanted to interview him before interviewing

Preview of: Missing

Annie's parents. She figured it was a necessary step of reopening the case that he had closed as a rooky police officer.

Alex was surprised at the initial response from the sheriff. He seemed offended that the Cincinnati police department was opening up his cold case.

She put out an invitation for him to become part of the team. She knew that if he felt threatened, he might turn into the worst of adversaries. This was something she did not need.

The Scots, Annie's parents, still lived in Loveland. They were second on Alex's list as she set out to learn more about that fateful day.

Alex knew that usually abductions were done by someone close to the family. She planned to ask Johnny to apply his computer skills to learn all he could about relatives and neighbors. She was especially interested in any that lived along the border of New York state and northern Pennsylvania or had property there.

She was personally planning to interview every person that had lived in Annie's neighborhood and still lived there. She would interview every relative that had been in the area when Annie disappeared. She was trying to control her bias about it being a male abductor. This was hard to do since more than eighty percent of abductions were by a male relative or someone close to the family.

Loveland Sheriff Evan Williams sat looking at the phone. He wondered why the Cincinnati Police were opening up Annie's cold case. He decided he wanted to know more and put in a call to one

Preview of: Missing

of his old buddies that was in the same office as the detective that had just called him.

He listened as his buddy Travis described the detective, he was curious about as "Cincinnati's black Annie Oakley." He was surprised at Travis's enthusiastic support of a female police officer. This Alex Evercrest must be a powerful presence. The fact that she had overcome multiple extremely violent personal attacks gave him some hope that she would solve the case that had haunted him throughout his career.

He hung up and called for Annie's cold case documents. He had not looked at them for several years and he wanted to refresh his memory. He always had bad memories when he reviewed the case. He considered it one of his top failures.

He decided that the best action was to first take a short bike ride along the Loveland bike trail and have a good lunch at his favorite sandwich shop. The ride would refresh him and give him new energy to once again relive the past that seemed like only yesterday. Once he got back, he would review the case that had been an albatross around his neck for his entire career.

Meanwhile Alex had invited Trey and Johnnie to have lunch at their favorite lunch spot. This was the restaurant where Alex had shot and killed the person who had thrown the young lady off an overpass onto the grill of a semitruck.

This killer had made the mistake of confronting her and pulling a gun that he never got to use because Alex put a bullet into his forehead as he brought the gun out from its holster.

Preview of: Missing

As she and her partner, Trey, got into the car she took a few moments to check that he was OK in her getting the both of them into Annie's cold case. She had become good friends with Trey. They both went to the same AA group each week. She often went to family dinners with Trey, his wife, and his son. She knew how the stress of getting into this case was already affecting her. She wanted to make sure Trey was OK.

Trey admitted that it did increase his stress but that for him it was different than before. He praised her for being a partner that recognized the stress but kept her cool. It inspired him and made things easier.

Alex thanked him and then led the way into the restaurant. She had gone there often enough that many of the staff knew her and always took her to the seat that she had when she had been attacked.

After lunch Alex took Trey up on his request to drive to Loveland. They had been issued a new car, and this was his first time to drive it.

She said she wanted to stop and buy some Toblerone and Ghirardelli chocolate on sale at Costgood. It would be a short stop on the way to Loveland.

When Trey asked what she had in mind, Alex replied that her mother had always told her that "you catch more flies with honey than with anything else."

Trey looked at her and replied that he would watch and figure it out.

Preview of: Missing

She took the car's instruction book out of the glove compartment and read about the operating features. She learned that the car could be started remotely. This would be a nice feature on cold days.

Alex dozed for a few minutes but came to full attention when Trey exited 71 and proceeded to Costco.

Alex went in and bought three pentagon boxes of Toblerone and three bags of Ghirardelli chocolate. On the way back to the car she told Trey how to start the car remotely. She also told him how to roll down the windows remotely.

She directed Trey to follow Union Cemetery Road toward Loveland.

A few moments later, Alex took in the Police building and expressed her opinion that the architect had used the windows to make the exterior look like the bars of a prison cell. The large parking lot was edged by a well-kept hedge and was almost totally empty. Parking would be no problem.

Sheriff Evan Williams watched as the car pulled into the parking lot. He knew immediately that it was a Cincinnati unmarked police car.

He closed Annie's file and checked to see that he had a fresh pot of coffee ready.

Trey chose the parking spot closest to the entrance.

Alex took one box and one bag of the chocolates and led the way in. Inside they were greeted by a tough looking deputy that

Preview of: Missing

sat behind an elevated counter. Alex and Trey both showed him their badge.

The deputy asked if they were armed.

Both Alex and Trey responded that they were.

The sergeant momentarily turned off the metal detector and had them enter.

Alex and Trey followed the deputy's instruction.

She stopped as she exited the scanner. She looked at the deputy and told him he needed a little sweetening. She gave him the five bar Toblerone box and asked him to share it with the other folks.

She took in his surprised look and his smile and quiet thank you.

She and Trey then turned to follow his instructions.

A female deputy met them as they turned toward the sheriff's office. She introduced herself as Melony and greeted them. She asked them to follow her to the chief's office.

Alex sensed that the escort by a female deputy was an intentional display by the Loveland sheriff. She asked Melony how long she had been on the force. Melony replied that the sheriff had hired her three years ago. Alex inferred that her guide was a signal by the sheriff that he supported equal treatment.

Alex was immediately on alert. She knew the sheriff had sounded unhappy that "his" cold case was being reopened by someone other than himself.

She was intent on enrolling him and making him a partner in the upcoming search for closure in Annie's case. She wanted to

Preview of: Missing

have his support and be on the resolution team. She did not want him to be a barrier.

Sheriff Williams stood up and took in the young black and good-looking detective and her partner. He was immediately captured by her composure and her greeting and her extended hand in which she held a bag of Ghirardelli chocolate. He wondered if she knew that these were one of his favorite chocolates.

He chuckled and asked whether he needed sweetening. He liked her immediately.

He stepped around his desk and shook her hand and then the hand of her partner. He was curious and ready to listen to what she had to say.

Alex looked over at the coffee pot and asked if she might get a cup. Trey said he would love one as well.

She watched as the sheriff took three plain white mugs and poured the coffee. She took her cup and then sat down on one of the chairs in front of the sheriff's desk. Trey did likewise.

The Sheriff took his mug in both hands and looked at Alex and asked why Annie's case was being reopened and why he had not been notified before its reopening.

Alex expressed the fact that if she were in his shoes she would probably be upset. She went on to explain that she had just finished with a trying case and had really been looking forward to a couple of months of boredom. She shared the fact that her on-line investigator had given her an analysis on Annie that he thought she should investigate. She had turned him down.

Preview of: Missing

Then a few hours later her Chief had called her into the office to listen to a Cincinnati Librarian about a young woman being held captive in the mountains in either northern Pennsylvania or southern New York. It was almost immediately clear that the story given to her by her analyst and that of the librarian were one and the same.

She shared that she had agreed with her Chief's opinion that having two sources identify the same case in the same week was a sign from above that she should look into the case.

Alex stopped for a moment and then expressed her desire for the Sheriff to be an integral part of the investigation. Alex pointed out that he might remember details that were not on the official report. He had lived it whereas she had to dig through paperwork to establish some connection and context for the case.

She specifically said she felt that his partnership would have a significant positive impact and help in finding out what happened and help solve the case.

Sheriff Williams looked at Alex for a long time. He had been surprised by her explanation about why the cold case was being opened. At that moment he felt hope that at long last the case would be solved.

He felt a shiver run down his back.

He looked at Alex and explained how this case had been an albatross around his neck. It had haunted him for his entire career. Every year he contacted Annie's family to see how they were doing.

Preview of: Missing

He admitted that he had been offended that someone else had decided to open up his cold case. He went on to say that Alex's invitation for him to participate convinced him that she was the right person to take a crack at closing the case.

He voiced his doubts but said he would be on her side.

Alex thanked the sheriff for the compliment and went on to ask him to review the case.

She asked him to go step by step, day by day through the case. She was sure there would be additional information that had not been in the report.

She also asked the sheriff to arrange interviews with Annie's parents and with each of the neighbors.

The sheriff asked her to call him Evan and agreed to set up the visits with everyone in the neighborhood.

Alex immediately sensed the emotional impact the case had on the sheriff. As he recalled the incident and added depth to the report, his voice often quavered, and it seemed that he periodically got tears in his eyes. He had been describing the events for almost an hour when he asked if they could take a break. He said he needed to get outside for some fresh air. He invited Alex and Trey to go with him.

The sheriff led them to a tan SUV and invited them to take a drive with him. Alex and Trey looked at each other and then accepted the invitation.

The interior of the SUV had light brown leather seats and was immaculate and had the smell of a brand-new car.

Preview of: Missing

Alex commented on the the quality of the ride.

The sheriff chuckled and thanked her and commented that the car was his wife's car. He said that he drove a forteen year old Honda Accord that was in the shop for its one hundred forty thousand mile tune up. He commented that he had splurged on new tires at Costgood.

The sheriff drove to the down town district. He parked the car in the street in front of his favorite Grill. He looked at Alex and asked if she wanted to take a walk. He didn't wait for a response but started a slow walk toward the river.

Alex wasn't sure where the little adventure was taking her but she agreed as she got out of the car. The Sheriff led the way back along Loveland Avenue until he got to the bridge. He walked to the center and looked down to the Little Miami river.

He looked at Alex and commented that he came to this spot almost everyday and almost everyday he thought of Annie. Alex listened as he went on tell her that every time someone drove by and honked their horn and waved, it saved him from the remorse he felt about that long cold case.

He said he would do everything possible to help her close it.

As if on que, a car drove past and honked their horn.

The sheriff smiled and asked if the two of them were ready for a cup of coffee at the Grill.

He led the way back and led the way in.

Alex came to a stop as she absorbed the atmosphere. A handwritten sign welcoming the customer was at the end of the counter

Preview of: Missing

closest to the door. A guitar enclosed in a glass covered wooden case was mounted on the wall above the bar at the far end. She knew of the Loveland bike trail and wondered what the two bicycles with white lights mounted on the wall signified.

A series of pictures and paintings led her eyes from the red bicycle up on the wall to an area to her right where additional paintings and pictures decorated the walls. A small wooden boat with oars was the final item that caught her attention. After taking it all in she proceeded to the eight-sided black topped table where the sheriff and Trey were sitting. She liked the feel of the place.

The sheriff commented that the Grill always had an impact on him too.

Coffee was ordered and Alex turned down the offer of a donut and opted for a banana.

The sheriff commented that he was burnt out on the interview about Annie but would make additional notes to share. He went on to say that he had not made his annual visit to Annie's parents and that he would arrange to do so. He invited both Alex and Trey to come with him.

Alex had accomplished what she had set out to do. Sheriff Evan Williams was now on her team, and he was taking the action that she needed him to.

The ride back to the Loveland police station was a quiet one. It was clear to Alex that they were all affected by the case.

Preview of: Missing

A few moments later the Sheriff parked next to her car. He looked over at her and commented that he had his mind on some Ghirardelli chocolate and asked if she wanted one before leaving.

Alex thanked him and let him know that she had also bought a bag for she and Trey.

She remarked that it would be great to get to talk to Annie's parents as soon as possible. She also requested his assistance in getting interviews set up with all the neighbors around and behind Annie's home.

He replied that he had accepted the chocolates because they were his favorites and he now he realized she had succeeded in bribing him. After a small chuckle, he said he would make the arrangements with Annie's parents and each of the neighbors that had lived there at the time when Annie went missing.

Alex commented that the candy approach was her mother's idea and that her mother got smarter with each passing year.

She shook the sheriff's hand and welcomed him onto the cold case solution team.

He replied that he would see her soon and that he felt they would make a good team.

She turned and opened the door to her car as Trey got into the driver's seat.

Trey commented that the meeting with the sheriff had been a resounding success. He complimented her in the chocolate candy approach and said he would push for her handle to be 'Cincinnati's sweet Annie Oakley."

Preview of: Missing

Alex replied that he had done enough in getting her labeled as the black Annie Oakley and he should leave well enough alone. She then dialed Martha, the librarian, and set up a meeting at two.

Trey commented that she seemed to be moving fast.

Alex replied that she intended to dig as deep as possible as quickly as possible. She said she felt that the person responsible might react negatively and she did not want to give that person time to react. She wanted that person to panic and make mistakes.

She suggested they stop at the Cheesecake Factory for lunch. She made the point that it was her treat. She knew that Trey was trying to stay on a tight budget because he was saving to buy a house.

Trey thanked her and told her that he owed her. He invited her to a Sunday lunch at his house. He knew his son, Nolan, enjoyed playing with Alex.

His wife, Leslie, was also fond of Alex. She credited Alex with helping him get control of his drinking habit. He also credited Alex.

He had turned her down when she had first invited him to join her in her visits to her AA meetings, but she always let him know when she was attending the meeting and asked if he would like to as well.

She had never pressured him, but he finally realized that she would continue to invite him until he at least went once.

Preview of: Missing

Alex had not pushed but always let him know when she was attending the meeting. Her approach worked. He spontaneously agreed to go with her a few weeks after many invitations. They now attended the meetings together on a regular basis. He found that the meetings and his partnership with Alex both contributed to his staying sober.

Alex accepted his invitation to a Sunday dinner at his place and responded that she would buy the desert of his choice at the Cheesecake Factory if he would let her have a spoonful.

Too soon a great lunch was over, and Alex had her spoonful. They headed back to the station.

The next stop on their way back was the Library.

Trey parked the car on the street and followed Alex into the Library. He took note that she was again carrying a bag of Ghirardelli candy.

They went to the main desk at the entrance and inquired about Martha. They were told to take the elevator to the third floor. Martha would be waiting for them and would lead them to her office.

Alex greeted Martha and gave her the chocolates after a brief hug. It was immediately apparent that Martha was touched and pleased as she volunteered that Ghirardelli chocolates were one of her favorite weaknesses.

Preview of: Missing

Martha led them back behind the third-floor reference desk to a small office where she opened her gift and offered them a choice of the gold, black, blue, or brown wrapped Ghirardelli. She picked one of the gold wrapped ones for herself.

Alex took a black wrapped one which she knew was plain dark chocolate. Trey took a blue wrapped one. The focus on the candy allowed Alex to lead the way into the discussion about Annie.

Martha recounted her story and as she went along, she remembered that the person who had shared the story about a mysterious cabin in the mountains had mentioned that it was north of the Pennsylvania finger lakes.

This piece of information excited Alex. She knew that Johnnie would be able to use the location to see if anyone in Annie's neighborhood had any property in that area. She knew that this information might be the big break she was looking for.

As she thought about this possibility, she finally opened her Ghirardelli and let the sweet dark chocolate melt slowly in her mouth.

Martha continued her story, but she still could not remember the name of the person who had told her the story. She apologized and pointed out that she talked to dozens of people a day and it seemed each had some personal story they wished to share.

She confessed that on somedays she would walk between the book stacks hiding from the library patrons so that she did not need to listen to them.

Preview of: Missing

Alex thanked her for the chocolate and the information. She made the point that the Finger Lake location was a very valuable clue that she was eager to explore. If it led somewhere, she promised to let Martha know.

As they left the Library, Alex suggested that they go and meet with Johnnie at his apartment and bring him up to date on what they had learned.

Her reliance on, Johnnie and his keen ability to cruise the internet and harvest the seeds that people had planted continued to grow. It was a relationship that was paying forward. She had put him on solid ground. He would for the rest of his time repay that by keeping her on that same solid footing.

Thank you for reading this far. To buy the book go to:

https://remwriter95.net/

Preview of: Missing

About the Author

Ronald E. Mueller
remwriter95@gmail.com

Ron grew up in what is now Flint River State Park in Southeast Iowa. The 170-year-old house Ron lived in is built into a hillside. It faces a 125-foot-high cliff towering over the little Flint River. The house and the land talked to him about; the passing of time, the struggle to conquer the land, the struggles people faced and the wonder of nature.

He climbed the cliffs, crawled into the caves, dove from the swimming rock, collected clams from the bottom of the pond, gigged and skinned frogs for their legs. He trapped muskrats for fur, hunted raccoon in the dead of night, and with only a stick hunted rabbits in the dead of winter.

His young life was outdoors, and nature tested him.

He walked to a one room stone schoolhouse uphill both ways. A stern but warm-hearted teacher, Mrs. Henry was instrumental in shaping his character as she shepherded him from the fourth to the eighth grade.

It was a great way to grow up.

Ron graduated from Burlington, High School, went to Vietnam in the Navy. He graduated from The University of South Florida with an master's degree in engineering, worked for thirty eight years for Procter and Gamble, traveled around the world thirty times.

He has remained happily married for more than fifty years. His daughter and his two sons are all successful and his three grandchildren have all graduated.

His wife has humored and supported him as he became a full time professional story teller.

He has come to realize that he is, what is known as, a Cozy writer. Excitement and adventure but little guts and gore. His heroine or hero live happily ever after.

His experiences inter-twined with snippets of fantasy lend themselves to the adventures he leads the reader through.

Books by Ron Mueller

Books By the Author

Fiction Series
The Alex Evercrest Series
    The River Front
    The Girl on The Grill
    Missing
    Maggot
    Racist
    Votive Candles
    Windy City
    Country Road
    Pool of Blood
    Sins of the Daughter
    Body Parts
    The Skull Collector
    The Vanishing
    The Shadow Fighter
    Moonshine
    Grief's Trajectory
    The Magic Touch
    Northern Lights
    Alex Evercrest Heroine
    Alex Evercrest Collection Two
    New Direction
    A Family Affair
    Disruption
    The St. Lebuinnus Church Murder

A Brian O'Neil Novel
    Hawaiian Phoenix
    Moon Curser
    Death Broker

The Problem Solver Series
    Solutions
    Drug Lords
    Border Crosser
    The Problem Solver Collection

Books by Ron Mueller

The Taelo Series
Taelo: The Early Years
Taelo: The Golden Feather
Taelo: Journey of Discovery
Taelo: Dangerous Passage
Taelo: Condor Clan Slingers
Taelo: Circumvention
Taelo: The Journey of Sages
Taelo: Collection
Taelo: Future Leaders Journey

A Taelo Story:
White Swan and Quiet Pheasant
The Child's Name
Floating Cloud
Quiet Rabbit
Busy Bee
Little Otter & Talking Wren
Broken Spear
Burley Bear & Meadow Flower
Taelo Story Collection

Science Fiction

The Savitar Series:
Journey's End
Savitar
Confluence
Savitar Series Collection

Bram Nielson Series
The Fold
The Message
Fold Wormhole
Negative Fold
Ripples in Time
Bram Nielson Collection

Single Science Fiction Books:
Current Past and Future
The Event
The Door
Viajante 7

Published by: Around the World Publishing LLC.

https://www.Remwriter95.net/

www.ingramcontent.com/pod-product-compliance
Lightning Source LLC
Chambersburg PA
CBHW072001070526
44583CB00015B/1285